MW00774306

THE ANTIETAM JOURNAL

Vol. III
September 2022

Kevin R. Pawlak
Editor

A Publication of the Antietam Institute

ISBN-13: 979-8-218-03876-2

The Antietam Journal is a biannual publication of the latest research, interpretation, and stories of the Maryland Campaign of September 1862 that highlights the participants involved—soldier and civilian—and the lasting impact of the campaign on American history.

The Antietam Institute was established in 2021 as a member-based, educational, and philanthropic 501(c)(3) non-profit organization. The Institute educates the public on the central role of the Maryland Campaign of 1862 and Battle of Antietam as a major turning point of the Civil War that directly resulted in the issuance of the preliminary Emancipation Proclamation. Antietam Institute-sponsored conferences, symposiums, publications, and leadership forums facilitate collaborative learning and knowledge exchange, create unique opportunities for discovery and inspire further historical research.

Manuscript Submissions

Send manuscript submissions to the editor at editor2@antietaminstitute.org. Feature articles should not exceed 10,000 words in length (including footnotes).

Cover image: Courtesy of Sharon Murray.

Table of Contents

The Editor's Column

One year ago, boxes of Volume I of *The Antietam Journal* arrived at the Antietam Institute's door. Now, here we are one year later with three volumes under our belt and a published book—*Brigades of Antietam*. It has been incredible to follow and rewarding to see the new amount of information and the varied interpretations of the events of the Maryland Campaign come out in print over the last year.

All of this is in time for the 160th anniversary of the Maryland Campaign. It is humbling to think we are already ten years removed from the sesquicentennial anniversary. Looking back, so much has changed for the better. Numerous new books and articles have been published to add to the growing conversation about the campaign, and to add more to your stack of books waiting to be read. Preservation and restoration efforts at Harpers Ferry, South Mountain, and Antietam have only bettered one of the best-preserved landscapes of the American Civil War. Antietam National Battlefield's Visitor Center is currently being upgraded. Both the bones of the building and the interpretative tools found inside will be new when it is reopened, adding another layer of conversation to Antietam's story and legacy. There has never been a better time than now to pick up a new Maryland Campaign book and visit the sites of the campaign to stand in the footsteps of the soldiers and civilians who experienced it firsthand. Their stories are worth remembering and retelling.

Volume III of *The Antietam Journal*—our 160th anniversary edition—contains new stories and different interpretations of old stories that we have grown accustomed to seeing over at least the last ten years.

Richard P. D'Ambrisi begins this edition by taking an interpreter's eye to Antietam National Battlefield. D'Ambrisi's work stresses the importance of learning and pondering the Battle of Antietam on the field itself. Whether you are an experienced Antietam visitor or if it is your first or second time visiting the battlefield, the questions he poses for pondering are important to keep in mind as you walk the hallowed ground of Antietam.

I decided to jump into these pages as an author, too. The story of A.P. Hill's march from Harpers Ferry to Sharpsburg on September 17 is often retold, perhaps more so than the actual fighting Hill's men did at Antietam. But during that fight, one story stands over all the others: did Hill's men go into battle wearing captured Union uniforms and flying

United States flags to deceive the enemy? Read on and discover my take on this repeated claim.

Another well-known fact about the Army of Northern Virginia in the Maryland Campaign found in campaign studies is that its strength waned considerably from the time it crossed the Potomac River until it crossed Antietam Creek less than two weeks later. Straggling plagued Robert E. Lee's army in Maryland. Did it plague the combat effectiveness of the Army of Northern Virginia as much as Lee said it did? For the first time, Russell Rich tries to quantify how much, or how little, the diminishing strength of the army impacted its ability to fight in Maryland.

In our "In Their Own Words" section, you will also find the lost words of Union cavalry commander Alfred Pleasonton, whose stance on one of his fellow generals changed from the first draft of his after-action report to the final draft.

Words would mean nothing when talking about Antietam if we did not remember the human side of the conflict. Joseph Stahl has reached into his collection of Civil War soldier images to bring one Antietam veteran's story off the pages.

J.O. Smith has once again provided a Maryland Campaign site for you to visit: Crampton's Gap. Even if you have been there numerous times, the battlefield's new trail makes a return visit a must. One cannot fully understand a battle without studying the ground. The terrain traversed by this trail will tell you much about the Battle of South Mountain, and the muscles in your legs might have something to say to you, too.

Our interviewer extraordinaire, Laura Marfut, sat down with Keith Snyder, Antietam National Battlefield's Chief of Resource Education and Visitor Services. Keith has a lot of sneak peeks about the work being done at the Visitor Center and what you can expect to see inside and outside of it when it reopens to the public later this year.

James A. Rosebrock—author of the Institute's upcoming *Artillery of Antietam*—took time out of his writing schedule to pen a review of a recent book about Antietam's Cornfield. It is exciting to see new books about the Maryland Campaign hitting the shelves.

Do not forget that you can be an author, too. If you are interested in writing for *The Antietam Journal*, fill out a proposal on our webpage: antietaminstitute.org/publications. I look forward to hearing from you, and seeing you on the battlefields of the Maryland Campaign.

Kevin R. Pawlak

Antietam Institute Announcements

Register Now for the Fall Conference: "Hidden in Plain Sight"

The Institute's second annual fall conference will be held on the weekend of October 21-23, 2022. This year's theme, "*Hidden in Plain Sight*," will examine some of the lesser-known aspects of the Maryland Campaign. It will feature Friday afternoon speakers, two Saturday field hikes, and two (shorter) Sunday field hikes. Six meals will also be included with ample time for interaction with presenters.

The Conference will be based at Shepherd's Spring Retreat Center, located near the battlefield. Out-of-town guests may reserve lodging at the conference center on a first-come, first-serve basis. Email us at: info@antietaminstitute.org.

Attendance is limited to 60 Institute members and the slots are filling up quickly. If you are intending to register, please consider doing so now so you do not miss out on a spot!

Antietam Institute Historical Research Center

We live in a digital age with thousands of sources at our fingertips. Unfortunately, there is rarely one place to go to find everything we are looking for. The Antietam Institute's website is now home to the Historic Research Center, a repository to collect and share digital copies of historical and contemporary material about the Battle of Antietam and the related Maryland Campaign.

The Historical Research Center has sources grouped into three categories: unit histories, images, and documents. This is a living resource that will continue to have sources added to it, so continue to visit the page to find more resources. Visit the Historical Research Center at https://antietaminstitute.org/hrc/s/HRC/page/welcome to find these valuable resources or to submit some of your own items for inclusion in the Historical Research Center.

Artillery of Antietam Coming Soon

Scheduled for release in the fall of 2022, the *Artillery of Antietam* is the first full-length treatment of the artillery fight on America's bloodiest day. Formatted like its companion book the *Brigades of Antietam*, *Artillery of Antietam* provides a detailed history of the over 100 batteries and their commanders who engaged in all the battles of the Maryland Campaign from South Mountain to Shepherdstown.

The book features specially created maps designed to clearly show terrain, battery deployment, and ranges of artillery. Details contained in dozens of letters written by artillery officers and soldiers to Ezra Carman add color and detail to the story. Written by James A. Rosebrock, a retired army officer and former chief of the Antietam Battlefield Guides, the book is the product of years of research and is destined to be the go-to source for everyone interested in learning the amazing story of the cannoneers of the blue and gray at Antietam. The book will be distributed to members at the Sergeant Major level and above.

Duryee Manuscript Preserved

The Antietam Institute has purchased a set of documents written more than a century ago by Jacob Duryee who led the 2nd Maryland Regiment in an attack at Burnside Bridge, including a 53-page account of his unit's attempt to take the bridge. This manuscript will be photocopied and placed in the Historical Research Center. The Institute wants to make sure these important documents are available to students of this battle, both online and in person. The manuscript will be donated to the Antietam National Battlefield Library later this year.

Sharpsburg Interpretive Plaza

The Institute presented our first pledged donation of $2,000 to the Sharpsburg Mayor and Town Council for the development of an interpretive plaza in the green space at the corner of Main and Church Streets. Initiated by the Town of Sharpsburg, this project will tell the story of Sharpsburg and the people who have lived there, even prior to the founding of the town in 1763. The town has received a matching grant for the first phase of the project.

For more information about both announcements, visit us online at www. antietaminstitute.org

Interpretive Themes for Experiencing Antietam National Battlefield
by Richard P. D'Ambrisi

Introduction

Antietam National Battlefield in Sharpsburg, Maryland, attracts thousands of visitors annually. The reasons for visiting the battlefield vary across a wide spectrum of interests. However, one essential element for a more rewarding experience during and after the visit, is the efficient use of interpretive themes. By fostering appreciation of Antietam National Battlefield as a historic resource and not just a travel destination, the park helps visitors delve deeper into the meaning of their experience and develop a sense of stewardship for the resource. Antietam National Battlefield is an excellent example of the classroom laboratory model of learning, whereby, after a reading of the literature, the student then steps onto the field to examine things firsthand. This essay will provide several examples of primary interpretive themes for visitors to consider during their visit followed by some critical thinking questions to stimulate further discussion after the battlefield tour.

Interpretive themes are the overarching, biggest stories about places and resources, based on their described significance. Interpretive themes forge intellectual and emotional connections between the interests of the visitor and the meanings inherent in the resource. Analogous to this, heritage interpretation is a communication process that guides visitors to discover meaning in objects, places, and landscape. This is especially applicable to Antietam where a museum, a collection of artifacts, a battlefield with numerous places to investigate, and a landscape that contributed in many ways to the outcome of the battle are all present.

People, in general, do not always remember rote facts. But they tend to retain themes, particularly if the theme is presented at the beginning of the experience. In other words, they will get the main idea even if they cannot remember the specifics. Successful interpretation builds connections between the tangibles or physical elements of the site to related intangible meanings or abstract concepts. This then leads to further connections to universal ideas or emotions that can contain meaning that will appeal to almost everyone. When these connections between tangible, intangible, and universal aspects are achieved, the visitor will have a more memorable experience that will often be retained for a lifetime.

The goal is to help visitors uncover the meaning and significance of this historic resource and motivate them to further action concerning Antietam National Battlefield. A visit to Antietam offers useful historical applications that can be explored via interpretive themes. The documentary record and physical presence on the site provide productive teaching tools that can be both informative and stimulating. Well thought-out interpretive themes also help to accomplish the overall mission of the site to educate and enlighten. In the case of Antietam, these themes may lead to further research on a topic of interest, volunteerism, and preservation efforts. Essentially, the fundamental purpose of an interpretive theme is to inspire and provoke people to broaden their horizons.

Structuring the visitor experience to a Civil War battlefield such as Antietam has a historical legacy. We can see this best by examining how visitors have sought meaning in three eras. During the years prior to 1890, visiting veterans were interested in recalling the personal dimensions of the bloodiest single day in American history. The National Cemetery and Private Soldier Monument gave them a focal point for this commemoration. The War Department from 1890 to 1933 added signs, markers, tablets, and roads to facilitate study of the military conduct of the battle so that groups of officers in training could benefit from their organized visits. Construction of the Observation Tower is an example of the open-air type of classroom. During this same period, groups were permitted to erect their own monuments on the battlefield, although to a much lesser degree than other national Civil War battlefield parks. Finally, since 1933, the National Park Service has maintained the site to its original 1862 appearance along with educational and audiovisual materials, a museum and library, brochures and maps, hiking trails, wayside exhibits on a tour road, special programs, and person-to-person Ranger interaction so that modern visitors can see the field with comparable knowledge to what their predecessors had. New themes to be explored further in the 2022 renovation of the Antietam Visitor Center are conflict, terror, survival, freedom, and memory.

An extensive examination of the motivation that brings visitors to Antietam is not within the scope of this essay. However, we can expect that varying amounts of preparation and effort are expended. Aside from the casual tourist seeking entertainment, we can also conclude that some visitors seek the opportunity not only to remember but to learn about and understand in a larger context what so many soldiers died for. Additionally, the physical condition of the battlefield landscape is often cited as a reason for visiting. The successful preservation of the battlefield to its 1862 appearance, sometimes unplanned especially during the early years of the battlefield's existence, is considered remarkable under present day standards. These visitor motivations are another way interpretive themes can be used to enhance any visit.

Interpretive Themes

This essay is a compilation of information and thus a comment on methodology is appropriate. The interpretive themes that follow were carefully selected from an Internet survey conducted by the author of credible websites related to Antietam National Battlefield. The interpretive theme statements chosen for this essay received minimal editing. While not every interpretive theme identified is included, the methodology employed ensures that only proven interpretive themes that will enhance the visitor's experience have been selected. (NOTE: Themes 1 through 8 provided below are the themes currently used by the National Park Service as a conceptual framework for telling the Antietam story in its entirety.)

1. A Turning Point: The Maryland Campaign of 1862, which culminated in the Battle of Antietam, was a major turning point of the Civil War and in American history.

2. The Single Bloodiest Day: The level of carnage, suffering, and human drama during and after the Battle of Antietam, the single bloodiest one-day battle in American history, has accorded it a prominent place in our national consciousness.

3. The Emancipation Proclamation and Abolition: The preliminary Emancipation Proclamation, issued as a direct result of the battle, changed the conflict from a war to restore the Union to a war that would also transform the nation by abolishing slavery and committed the country to redefining the freedoms espoused in its founding documents.

4. Tactics, Terrain, Technology, and Leadership: Tactics, terrain, technology, and leadership directly affected the outcome of the Battle of Antietam.

5. Impact of the Battle on the Local Population: The Battle of Antietam had a major impact on the local civilian population.

The Burnside Bridge and stone wall on the southern end of the Antietam battlefield showing a glimpse of the landscape that shaped the battle here. (Richard P. D'Ambrisi)

6. Legacy and Evolving Values: The varied and continuing efforts of commemoration by succeeding generations illustrate society's evolving values regarding the Civil War and the legacy of the Battle of Antietam.

7. Revolution in Medical Care: Dr. Johnathan Letterman and other leaders in the medical corps created the foundation of modern battlefield medicine when faced with the immense number of casualties at Antietam including development of the American system of triage, the ambulance corps, and forward aid stations.

8. Soldier's Experience: Individual soldiers were deeply impacted by their unique experiences from enlistment to battle and through homecoming and remembrance.

9. Battlefield Photography: The photographs taken at Antietam within days after the battle were the first to publicly display the carnage and horrors of the American Civil War.

10. Antietam National Cemetery: Dedicated in 1867 as the final resting place for Union soldiers who fell at Antietam, the Cemetery continues to serve as a memorial to honor military sacrifice.

11. Solemnity of the Site: Antietam National Battlefield provides an

opportunity to experience a solemn, peaceful, and reverent space, where one can reflect upon the sacrifices of the fallen and the implications of the battle.

12. Natural Resources: To help protect park natural resources like air quality, soil, forests, plants, streams, and wildlife, a team of National Park Service scientists with the National Capital Region Inventory and Monitoring Network is continually assessing conditions at Antietam National Battlefield.

13. Logistics: There were an estimated 500 artillery pieces at the Battle of Antietam along with numerous wagons, horses, and mules to transport large amounts of ammunition, equipment, and supplies.

14. Strategic Impacts: The Battle of Antietam enabled the Union army to repel the first Confederate invasion of the North, kept England and France from actively supporting the Confederacy by remaining neutral, lifted sagging Union morale, and may have helped Lincoln's Republican Party in the congressional midterm elections of November 1862.

Critical Thinking Questions

Critical thinking questioning is the basis for the analysis of facts to form a judgment. A critical thinker asks questions that aim to encourage deeper understanding of a particular subject. There may not be one absolute correct answer, but rather different perspectives on what that answer might be. What follows here are several examples of critical thinking questions that pertain to the Maryland Campaign of 1862. These questions were created or edited by the author and are intended to stimulate further discussion beyond the basic facts of the battle.

1. Why was the Battle of Antietam a significant turning point in the Civil War and American history?

2. Do you think the Union and Confederate generals knew how important the Battle at Antietam would be during the Civil War? Why or why not?

3. What effect do you feel the Battle of Antietam had on the public's perceptions and attitudes about the war?

4. Identify and assess the effect of the physical landscape and geography on the conduct of military operations during the Maryland Campaign of 1862. Consider things like crop fields, wooded areas, roads, fences, bridges, depressed and raised land features, rock formations, stone walls, mountains, and rivers. What impact did the landscape and geography have on troop movements, avenues of approach and retreat, weapons

deployment, observation, fields of fire, command and control communications, and support logistics? Give some examples. Climb the Observation Tower for a panoramic view of the battlefield.

5. Why did President Lincoln lose faith in Maj. Gen. George McClellan's command ability after the battle?

6. Why does General McClellan today not hold the same prominence as Abraham Lincoln?

7. Why is nurse Clara Barton considered a hero at Antietam? Were her actions typical of a woman in the Civil War era? How else did Clara Barton participate in the American Civil War? Did other women give aid to the soldiers at Antietam? If so, who were they and why did they help?

8. The Battle of Antietam was fought over a large area of land. Some parts of the engagement occurred simultaneously to each other while others occurred separate from other actions. What might have happened if the principal fighting had occurred simultaneously all along the battle line? As a commander, how would you manage a full-frontal assault? Do some research on rifled weaponry and the impact on Napoleonic, Scott's, and Hardee's military tactics.

9. Union troops arrived from Washington, DC, and Confederate troops arrived from Virginia. What do you think the impact of marching so many miles had on the troops and the outcome of the battle?

10. There were six senior commanders and numerous subordinate officers killed during the battle. What impact did this have on command and control of troops and the outcome of the battle?

11. What do you think were factors that contributed to neither army renewing the fighting on September 18, the day immediately after the battle?

12. What role did military flags play in the Battle of Antietam? Why were flags so important during the Civil War?

13. Think about witness trees, monuments, mortuary cannon, the Medal of Honor, and the National Cemetery. How do each of these play a role in commemorating what occurred at the Battle of Antietam?

14. Do some research on the weather conditions in western Maryland during September 1862. How did the weather affect roads, weapons performance, soldiers camping, cooking, medical care, and animals used for military purposes? Consider temperature, humidity, precipitation, cloud cover, winds, hours of daylight, and moonlight. Create an hourly weather timeline for September 16, 17, and 18, 1862.

Antietam National Cemetery on Memorial Day. (Richard P. D'Ambrisi)

15. How did the Emancipation Proclamation affect society in the short-term and the long-term?

16. What are some of the advantages of parking at each tour stop and walking the guided trails?

17. What aspects concerning the Battle of Antietam are of interest to you? How would you research more information?

18. What are the missions of the National Park Service and Save Historic Antietam Foundation at this site?

19. How can you, your family, and friends participate and become more involved with Antietam National Battlefield?

Summary

The overall objective of this essay has been to provide the visitor to Antietam National Battlefield a selection of interpretive themes and critical thinking questions to enhance their experience and help make their visit more enriching and memorable. I have provided basic definitions of historic site interpretation and detailed the importance of interpretive themes as a foundation for the reader to explore the Antietam battlefield. Regardless of how much time is available to be in the park, using the heritage interpretation tools offered in this essay will open new areas of interest to pursue. This new awareness presents a unique and powerful opportunity for visitors to interact with, reflect upon, and immerse themselves in the meaning and values of one of the most significant battles of the American Civil War. Finally, I have included some photographs from today's battlefield as examples of on-site assets that may enhance your understanding and interpretation of what occurred near a small farming community in western Maryland on September 17, 1862. Enjoy your visit and come back often.

Deception in the Forty-Acre Cornfield?
by Kevin R. Pawlak

It's the stuff of legend. Eight thousand soldiers of the Army of the Potomac's Ninth Corps marched towards the weakened right flank of the Army of Northern Virginia on the afternoon of September 17, 1862.[1] They seized high ground south of Sharpsburg, Maryland and even entered the outskirts of the town, poised to deal Gen. Robert E. Lee's army a crippling, decisive defeat. Then, Maj. Gen. A.P. Hill's division arrived south of town to attack the Federals after a march of over a dozen miles from Harpers Ferry. The two opposing forces met in a 40-acre cornfield owned by Joseph Sherrick on the south end of the Antietam battlefield. In the fight, Federal soldiers claimed that Hill's men were clad in blue uniforms and flew the Stars and Stripes above their battle lines, thus giving the Confederates the upper hand. The bloodiest single day battle in American history ended, and Lee's army was preserved, thanks in part to this confusion and misperception by the Union troops. Though some historians have rightly questioned this claim, many others have taken it as fact, and it has been often retold in the histories of the Battle of Antietam.[2]

Several factors contributed to make Antietam's Sherrick cornfield a uniquely confusing place for Civil War combat to take place. Weather, terrain, the corn itself, and the natural chaos of nineteenth century warfare conspired to make false perceptions a reality in the minds of those who fought there. When the action began there at 4:20 p.m., the sun was already beginning its descent over the western horizon, meaning it set in the faces of the Federals. Sunset was just under two hours away. The blinding sun, which grew worse as it continued to set, made making out clear details about opposing lines of battle difficult. Additionally,

---

1 The engaged statistic of Ninth Corps troopsinvolved in Antietam's Final Attack comes from John David Hoptak, *The Battle of Antietam, September 17, 1862* (Western Maryland Interpretive Association), 70.

2 See Carol Reardon and Tom Vossler, *A Field Guide to Antietam: Experiencing the Battlefield through Its History, Places, and People* (Chapel Hill, NC: The University of North Carolina Press, 2016), 262-63 for an example of historians who expressed doubt about the story. James V. Murfin, *The Gleam of Bayonets: The Battle of Antietam and the Maryland Campaign of 1862* (New York: Thomas Yoseloff, 1965), 284, and Stephen W. Sears, *Landscape Turned Red: The Battle of Antietam* (New York: Houghton Mifflin Co., 1983), 288-89, are two examples of this oft-told story being repeated.

winds of only two miles per hour did little to dissipate thick battle smoke or keep flags aloft. Instead, with such little wind, the banners of both armies limply drooped on the staffs to which they were tied.[3]

Additionally, the irregular, up-and-down terrain in the cornfield limited participants' views of their enemy. The head-high corn and battle smoke impaired vision even further, as attested to by soldiers of both sides. Brigadier General Maxcy Gregg's brigade historian remembered, "So dense was the corn that the lines sometimes approached within thirty or forty yards of each other before opening."[4] The green 16th Connecticut saw even less—just twelve feet in front of them once the shooting started.[5] Henry J. Spooner in the neighboring 4th Rhode Island noted "the thick, high grown corn served largely to conceal [the enemy] from us, but where their position was demonstrated by their sharply challenging rifles."[6]

Despite these visual handicaps, Federal soldiers were convinced Confederate soldiers dressed in Union blue, flying recently captured United States flags, descended upon them and gained the upper hand by their deception. There are multiple contemporary accounts by Union soldiers claiming this deception. A soldier in the 23rd Ohio wrote six days after the battle, "The rebels were seen coming down upon us, but were mistaken for our men, they having our flag flying and was dressed in our uniform."[7] One Connecticut private named Culver told his story to a newspaper correspondent immediately after the battle:

> The enemy commenced a flanking movement, in which they were nearly successful in accomplishing, having treacherously displayed the U.S. colors, until ready to grapple with the foe. Culver relates that the brigade received the fire of the rebels before warned of their presence. The wretches were calling on

3 Joseph L. Harsh, *Sounding the Shallows: A Confederate Companion for the Maryland Campaign of 1862* (Kent, OH: The Kent State University Press, 2000), 19-20.
4 J.F.J. Caldwell, *The History of a Brigade of South Carolinians* (Philadelphia, PA: King & Baird Printers, 1866), 46.
5 D. Scott Hartwig, "Who Would Not Be a Soldier: The Volunteers of '62 in the Maryland Campaign," in Gary W. Gallagher, ed., *The Antietam Campaign* (Chapel Hill, NC: The University of North Carolina Press, 1999), 162.
6 Henry J. Spooner, *The Maryland Campaign with the Fourth Rhode Island* (Providence, RI: Rhode Island Soldiers and Sailors Historical Society, 1903), 23.
7 "Watts," 23rd Ohio Infantry, 9th Corps, "Watts" to Dealer, September 23, 1862, in *Cleveland Plain Dealer*, September 30, 1862.

them not to fire upon their own friends. At the point of attack, they lowered their standard and hoisted the rebel ensign in its place...[8]

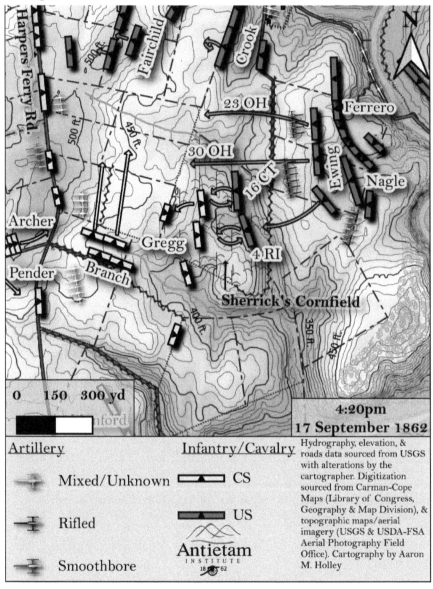

A.P. Hill's attack into Sherrick's Cornfield (Aaron Holley)

---

8 "Our Connecticut Regiments," *Hartford Courant*, September 22, 1862.

These claims were not restricted to newspaper correspondence. Less than one week after the battle, two officers claimed Confederate trickery in their official reports. The 23rd Ohio's Maj. James Comly reported:

> About the same time I discovered that the Thirtieth Regiment was still in the corn-field, and that they had opened fire upon what I supposed was our own troops, advancing from the left. It seems proper to state that this supposition did not rest entirely upon the fact that the enemy had uniforms similar to ours, and which (I have since been informed by a prisoner) were taken at Harper's Ferry, but upon the fact that they used the national colors on the occasion.[9]

Colonel Joseph B. Curtis of the 4th Rhode Island similarly testified that the flags carried by the Confederates rather than the uniforms donned by them created the most uncertainty. A "sharp musketry from the front" struck Curtis' men, "but as the enemy showed the national flag (the corn concealing their uniform)," Curtis ordered his men to stop shooting at the apparent friendly force in their front. He sent an officer forward "to ascertain who was in our front." It was quickly discovered to be the enemy.[10] Postwar accounts repeating these stories solidified the Federals' collective perception that they had been duped on Antietam's southern flank. For them, it was very real. Their perception became their reality.[11]

Confusion over the enemy's uniforms and flags was nothing new to Civil War combat by September 1862. From the war's first major conflict at Bull Run, the similar looking Stars and Bars and Stars and Stripes hanging limp on their flagstaffs on a near windless day halted the trigger fingers of countless soldiers as they sought to determine the identity of soldiers at the end of their muzzles. In response to this confusion, Confederate General P.G.T. Beauregard proposed a change, "to adopt for my command a 'Battle flag,' which would be Entirely different from any State or Federal flag." His determination set in motion the creation of the Confederate battle flag. On November 24, 1861, orders emanated

---

9 *War of the Rebellion: The Official Records of the Union and Confederate Armies* (Washington, DC: GPO, 1887), Series 1, vol. 19, pt. 1, 468. Hereafter cited as *OR*, all citations from Series 1 unless otherwise stated.
10 Ibid., 456.
11 See Jacob D. Cox, "The Battle of Antietam" in *Battles and Leaders of the Civil War* (New York: The Century Co., 1887), 2:655, and Spooner, *Maryland Campaign*, 23.

from Beauregard's headquarters dictating "in the event of an action with the enemy, the new battle flag recently issued to the regiments of this army corps will alone be carried on the field. Meantime regimental commanders will accustom their men to the flag, so that they may be thoroughly acquainted with it."[12] Beauregard's orders to become familiar with the new flag were not for the benefit of the enemy. Instead, Confederates flew the new flag on the field to differentiate themselves from their enemy, aid their commanders in locating friendly troops, and prevent deadly friendly fire incidents.

From a broader standpoint, Confederate politicians could not stomach flying an enemy's flag on the battlefield to deceive their enemy while keeping theirs cased. Virginia governor John Letcher espoused this idea to the state's General Assembly in 1862. Regarding certain "violations" of the United States Army thus far in the war, Letcher asked:

> What civilized nation would not blush to conceal its own flag, the emblem of its nationality and honor, and hoist on the battle-field the flag of its enemy, in order to decoy that enemy into a murderous fire, and then glory in the meanness of the deception and cowardice of the act? What ancient or modern nation ever used a flag of truce to decoy an enemy in battle other than the United States of America? Let history record the disgrace and brand the infamy upon their brow for all time to come.

By Letcher's standards, decoying the enemy with the use of their flag was an act of cowardice, one that only the United States resorted to but one that the Confederacy must not.[13]

The replacement of the Stars and Bars with the Confederate battle flag did not end friendly fire incidents between Confederate units on the battlefield. During the Battle of Gaines Mill on June 27, 1862, Gregg's South Carolina brigade, one of the brigades at the center of Antietam's flag controversy, marched onto the field. The brigade, along with the rest of A.P. Hill's division, received their second bunting issue of the battle flag prior to this engagement. Some units of Gregg's brigade may have carried them onto the field on June 27, though it is known that the 1st

---

12 John M. Coski, *The Confederate Battle Flag: America's Most Embattled Emblem* (Cambridge, MA: The Belknap Press of Harvard University Press, 2005), 8-10.
13 *OR*, vol. 51, pt. 2, 583.

South Carolina continued marching under its blue palmetto flag.[14] Regardless, artillerymen under Maj. Gen. Thomas J. "Stonewall" Jackson's command had trouble distinguishing Gregg's identity. The gunners signaled Gregg, "but receiving no reply, and being unable to distinguish our colors or uniform, had fired upon us for the enemy." Friendly fire incidents still occurred, and troops could similarly still confuse the enemy for friends.[15]

Despite Beauregard's best intentions to mitigate mix-ups on the battlefield, the chaotic, fluid, and smoke-obscured nature of Civil War battlefields ensured more confusion about a body of troops' identity. During the June 30, 1862, Battle of Glendale, at least two instances of Confederate deception were recorded within days of the battle. The 12th New York Infantry's Lt. Col. Robert M. Richardson watched his men fire on the enemy's colors with great effectiveness, noting his men dropped the enemy's flag four separate times. At one point in the action, they even "displayed the American colors," Richardson recorded.[16]

Union brigade commander Cuvier Grover noted a similar instance, though this time the conditions on the battlefield plagued his perception. It was "nearly sunset," Grover wrote. Battle smoke clogged the vision of the fight's participants. "On the left, somewhat nearer to our position," said Grover, "a column of infantry was moving by the flank to the right. Their colors were furled, and they wore the uniform of our troops, and were believed to be a regiment from the left of the Excelsior Brigade, moving to re-enforce the right of our position." The mystery formation approached Grover's men "and fired a volley upon us." That volley did not convince Grover that it was the enemy. He ordered his men to fall back and not return fire. Once he placed his men in a safe location, "I returned to assure myself of the facts of the case, and rode within about 100 yards of their colors, which had become partially loosened from the staff. It was a rebel regiment, and gave me a volley as soon as I was observed."[17] Furled colors, fading sunlight, and dark powder smoke made the surest man uncertain of formations facing him.

Confederate uniforms also conspired to conceal troops' identity on the

---

14 *Echoes of Glory: Arms and Equipment of the Confederacy* (Alexandria, VA: Time-Life Books, 1996), 248; Glenn Dedmondt, *The Flags of Civil War South Carolina* (Gretna, LA: Pelican Publishing Company, 2000), 46.
15 Caldwell, *History of a Brigade*, 15.
16 *OR*, vol. 11, pt. 2, 329.
17 Ibid., 123-24.

Civil War battlefield due to their color, though this was not the intent. A member of the 83rd New York Infantry wrote that at the Battle of Antietam, the enemy's "uniform being of the color of the dirt, we could not see them very well."[18] Gorham Coffin in the 19th Massachusetts agreed. "The rebels wear a sort of grey or brown uniform so much the collor [sic] of the trees that we can hardly see their lines."[19] Lastly, Capt. Frederick Seymour of the 7th Ohio Infantry said the enemy's "rags, were so near the color of the ground that at first it was difficult to see where they were, but we soon learned, for the leaden hail came thick and fast," a sure sign of the enemy's location.[20]

Confusion was a common factor on any Civil War battlefield. There are a host of reasons why units thought their enemies were friends or believed their friends to be enemies. A deeper examination of A.P. Hill's troops, the uniforms they wore, and the flags they flew, is required to determine the validity of Federal claims of deception.

Though numerous Union soldiers wrote of the deadly misperception in the Sherrick cornfield, this author has located no Confederate accounts that admit to this tactic during the battle. Following the surrender of the Federal garrison at Harpers Ferry, the victorious Confederate troops, especially those of A.P. Hill's division, found a cornucopia of captured supplies to take for their own purposes. A member of the 16th North Carolina quickly noted the differences in appearance between the vanquished enemy and his victorious comrades. "The enemy was spotlessly dressed in brand-new uniforms, shoes and buttons, and gold and silver trappings glistening in the morning sun, while we were almost naked; a great many of us without shoes, without even a faded emblem on our ragged coats to tell even rank or official command."[21] Fortunately for the men of Hill's division, which Jackson left behind to gather the captured supplies and parole the prisoners, they had the best and longest chance to replace their "ragged coats" with new,

18 John W. Jaques, *Three Years' Campaign of the Ninth, N. Y. S. M., during the Southern Rebellion* (New York: Hilton & Co., 1865), 113-14.
19 Gorham Coffin to Father and Sister, September 23, 1862, Gorham Coffin Pension File, National Archives and Records Administration.
20 Frederick A. Seymour to Editor, October 13, 1862, in Richard J. Staats, *A Grassroots History of the American Civil War*, vol. 2, *The Bully Seventh Ohio Volunteer Infantry* (Bowie, MD: Heritage Books, Inc., 2003), 89.
21 Benjamin B. Cathey, "Sixteenth Regiment," in Walter Clark, ed., *Histories of the Several Regiments and Battalions from North Carolina in the Great War 1861-'65* (Raleigh, NC: E.M. Uzzell, 1901), 1:760.

blue ones.

The Confederates who captured Harpers Ferry did not look the part of a conquering army. "We were nearly naked, had not had time to wash clothes," recalled the 19th Georgia's John Keely.[22] Union onlookers agreed. Lieutenant Henry B. Curtis Jr. called the Confederates "rugged & shoeless and guns rusty and dirty."[23] In their condition, it was difficult for the Confederate soldiers to restrain themselves. "We immediately replenished our wardrobes from those of the enemy," Keely wrote.[24] Andrew Wardlaw, 14th South Carolina Infantry, licked his lips at the Federal supply stocks. "The whole ground was dotted with their tents," he recorded. Discarded Confederate uniforms also "pretty well covered" the ground "in places...which our soldiers had thrown off, substituting new ones. I got a good Yankee overcoat for myself & one for Wiley, which later came in very well as he lost his."[25] Enough southerners swapped their uniforms for Federal ones that the 14th Tennessee's Robert T. Mockbee recalled when Brig. Gen. James J. Archer's brigade began its march for the Antietam battlefield on the morning of September 17, "*but for the tattered Battle flags* [they] might have been taken for a brand new Brigade from Boston so completely were they clothed in Yankee uniforms" [emphasis added].[26]

Confederate officers tried to control the free-for-all. Mockbee's 14th Tennessee received the task of guarding "one of the large buildings where were stored vast quantities of Quartermaster supplies" in Harpers Ferry on September 16 to prevent Confederate troops from walking off with whatever they could grab. However, Mockbee and his comrades shunned their duties and instead spent the day "appropriating whatever might suit the fancy of any one individual to his own personal use."[27] Union and Confederate soldiers "nearly all traded canteens & made each other presents, & cut off buttons from their coats and gave to each other," wrote

---

22 Capt. John Keely, "Civil War Diary Relates Record of Famous Atlanta Company," BV 127, Fredericksburg & Spotsylvania National Military Park.

23 D. Scott Hartwig, *To Antietam Creek: The Maryland Campaign of September 1862* (Baltimore, MD: Johns Hopkins University Press, 2012), 564.

24 Keely, "Civil War Diary," BV 127, FSNMP.

25 Andrew B. Wardlaw, "Diary of Andrew B. Wardlaw," 14th South Carolina Infantry File, Antietam National Battlefield.

26 Robert T. Mockbee, "The 14th Tennessee Infantry Regiment," in *Civil War Regiments*, vol. 5, no. 1 (Campbell: CA: Savas Publishing Company, 1995), 21.

27 Ibid.

one New Yorker.[28] Members of the 7th and 18th North Carolina regiments updated their Springfield muskets for Springfield rifles, "a more effective weapon at longer range."[29]

One coveted item that Union soldiers were not eager to give up or trade were their colors. These flags rest at the center of the story that Confederates purposefully used the spoils of the surrender of Harpers Ferry to deceive the enemy on the south end of the battlefield. Thus, it is important to establish what happened to these surrendered flags between the surrender of the Federal garrison on the morning of September 15 and the afternoon of September 17.

In the aftermath of the Seven Days' Campaign, orders went out from Army of Northern Virginia headquarters "prohibiting commands that fell under the control of the Army of Northern Virginia from carrying flags of design other than that of the Virginia army," an edict that limited Confederate units to flying only a single battle flag, likely to avoid confusion and friendly fire incidents.[30] Occasionally, exceptions were made, as in the case of the 3rd North Carolina Infantry at Antietam. On October 5, 1862, the regiment's major, Stephen D. Thruston, wrote to his state's governor, Zebulon Vance, returning the state colors in possession of his regiment to North Carolina. Thruston presented Vance with a history of the flag. "When the regiment was first attached to the army before Richmond the Confederate battle-flag was issued to it and all other colors ordered to be discarded. Previous to the battles in Maryland, however, our colonel, at the request of both officers and men, once more unfurled our North Carolina colors...and, in addition to our battle-flag, carried this into the engagement at Sharpsburg."[31] However, it was not only protocol for regiments to return their state colors to their respective states but also those captured on the field of battle.

Also in the summer of 1862, the policy of what Confederate armies did with captured enemy flags took form; these flags went up the chain of command to the War Department and the Secretary of War. The process was not immediately commenced upon the flags' capture but

---

28 Hartwig, *To Antietam Creek*, 564. "Canteens" is outlined in the original source.
29 J.S. Harris, "Seventh Regiment, in Walter Clark, ed., *Histories of the Several Regiments and Battalions from North Carolina in the Great War 1861-'65*, vol. 1 (Raleigh, NC: E.M. Uzzell, 1901), 372; William H. McLaurin, "Eighteenth Regiment," in Clark, ed., ibid., 32.
30 *Echoes of Glory: Confederacy*, 250.
31 *OR*, vol. 51, pt. 2, 632.

instead as soon as hostilities slowed enough to allow for the transfer.[32]

During the June 27, 1862, Battle of Gaines' Mill, Col. Micah Jenkins' Palmetto Sharpshooters captured the regimental flag of the 16th Michigan Infantry. Following the conclusion of the Seven Days Campaign, Jenkins appealed to his superiors to keep the flag and present it to South Carolina's governor. The request made its way from Maj. Gen. James Longstreet to General Lee to Secretary of War George Randolph. On July 18, Lee informed Longstreet that Randolph approved Jenkins' request. Three days later, Longstreet told Jenkins and the flag went to South Carolina's capitol.[33]

Surely, Confederates at Harpers Ferry did not have time to send the captured colors to Richmond immediately. Then the question must be asked: what happened to the captured flags from Harpers Ferry?

The Harpers Ferry garrison consisted of 13 infantry battalions and regiments, meaning there were as many as 13 national flags up for grabs once the garrison surrendered. However, as stated above, the captured Federals did not part with their flags as easily as they did some of their other possessions. Of the 13 regiments that surrendered, three acknowledged they surrendered their colors, eight claim to have prevented their flags from falling into enemy hands by a number of different and bold measures, while the status of the flags of the remaining two regiments—the 1st and 3rd Maryland Potomac Home Brigade— remains unclear.

Immediately after the surrender, the Union regiments marched to Bolivar Heights to lay down their arms and colors and receive their paroles. The victorious Confederates went hunting for food, clothing, and other necessities while trying to grab souvenirs of war, including Union flags. After the 87th Ohio stacked its arms at the foot of the heights, "The Johnnies immediately put a guard over them," remembered the regiment's Demas L. Coe. The Confederate officer charged with guarding the 87th Ohio inquired where its colors were. "He was told we did not have any," said Coe. "Of course, he knew better, and was very indignant and made many threats, but failed to learn of their

---

32 See ibid., vol. 11, pt. 3, 674, for an example of this, where Lee sent Secretary of War George Randolph "the regimental colors of the Twelfth Regiment New York Volunteers, taken by General Longstreet's division in the late battles before Richmond."
33 Ibid., vol. 11, pt. 3, 644; ibid., vol. 51, pt. 2, 595.

whereabouts."[34] Other Confederates did not turn up empty handed and snagged the flags of the 12th New York State Militia, the 126th New York, and the 60th Ohio.[35] Hill's men did seize other flags, likely guidons and flank markers. The regimental historian of the 115th New York saw "a couple of rebel officers bearing at least twenty flags taken from various regiments" while another Federal saw "nearly a score of others" fall into enemy hands.[36]

While the Confederates made off with many lesser flags, most of the surrendered infantry regiments managed to keep their large national and state colors out of enemy hands. The members of the 125th New York ripped their flag apart and hid the pieces among the regiment's members.[37] Both the 115th New York and 9th Vermont stripped their flags from the poles and placed the oilcloth covers over the naked pole, "which no doubt caused the enemy to think the flags were beneath." The ruse worked. Two members of the 115th New York wrapped a flag around each of their bodies underneath their uniform while the color

"Soldiers Were Smashing Their Muskets."
(Brattleboro Reformer, *August 23, 1895)*

34 Demas L. Coe, "Harper's Ferry Surrender: Saving the Colors of the 87th Ohio," *National Tribune*, July 16, 1908.
35 "Important News from Maryland," *New York Times*, September 18, 1862; Arabella M. Willson, *Disaster, Struggle, Triumph: The Adventures of 1000 'Boys in Blue,' from August, 1862, to June, 1865* (Albany, NY: The Argus Company, 1870), 333; "Battleflags Returned," *National Tribune*, September 22, 1898. The state colors of the 60th Ohio were not returned to the state until September 1898.
36 James H. Clark, *The Iron Hearted Regiment: Being an Account of the Battles, Marches and Gallant Deeds Performed by the 115th Regiment N. Y. Vols.* (Albany, NY: J. Munsell, 1865), 24; Willson, *Disaster*, 333.
37 Ezra D. Simons, *A Regimental History: The One Hundred and Twenty-Fifth New York State Volunteers* (New York: Ezra D. Simons, 1888), 33.

bearer of the 32nd Ohio encircled himself in both flags.[38] The company flag, a smaller standard, for Company B, 65th Illinois escaped detection because Mrs. Jackson Moore, whose husband served in the company, "donned it as an under garment and escaped to the Union line."[39]

In order to keep their schemes a secret, the hiding or dismemberment of the Union colors were closely held to the chests of a few men. The soldiers of the 87th Ohio believed their flag was lost. On September 17, 1862, while the Battle of Antietam raged, the regiment was marching to a parole camp. During the march, it paused to rest. A handful of Ohioans wandered into a nearby woodlot and returned "with a rough pole, when our color-bearer surprised us by undressing and unwrapping our colors from around his body, and, tying it on the pole, raised it up with a whoop, 'Here is your colors, boys.'" Loud cheers greeted the reveal. "Oh, how we hugged and kissed that flag," said one Ohioan.[40]

The terms of surrender agreed upon between the two armies allowed officers to retain their sidearms and personal baggage.[41] Colonel Frederick D'Utassy, one of the garrison's brigade commanders, used that term to smuggle the flags of his regiments along with his personal belongings.[42] No matter how they did it, most of the Harpers Ferry regiments managed to sneak their flags out of their camps and thus deprived Hill's division from sending them to Richmond as trophies or carrying them into the Battle of Antietam.

Even if Hill's men had managed to capture more than two sets of regimental colors to carry them into battle and deceive the enemy, it seems doubtful that they would do so. As is previously mentioned, Civil War battlefields were chaotic environments with limited visibility. While Hill's men could have fooled Federal soldiers by wearing blue uniforms and flying the United States flag, that would make them more likely to be shot at by their own infantry and artillery. Regardless, the point is moot, as evidence exists regarding what uniforms Hill's men wore into the Battle of Antietam and what flags they fought under despite their spoils of Union uniforms and flags from Harpers Ferry.

38 George L. Kilmer, "The Ninth Vermont," *Brattleboro Reformer* (Brattleboro, VT), August 23, 1895; Clark, *Iron Hearted Regiment*, 24-25; E. Z. Hays, ed., *History of the Thirty-second Regiment Ohio Veteran Volunteer Infantry* (Columbus, OH: Cott & Evans, 1896), 33-34.
39 "Fly Your Flags," *The Rock Island Argus* (Rock Island, IL), September 14, 1886.
40 Coe, "Harper's Ferry Surrender," *National Tribune*, July 16, 1908.
41 *OR*, vol. 19, pt. 1, 980.
42 Ibid., 599, 606.

As Hill's division began its march to Sharpsburg on the morning of September 17, Robert Mockbee of the 14th Tennessee specifically noted that, despite their new, blue uniforms, Mockbee's comrades marched under "tattered Battle flags..." Once Hill's men came nearer to the battlefield, the echoes of gunfire reached their ears, clearly indicating what the men were about to face. The march was made with haste and little rest. Whenever they did rest briefly and then rise up to continue the march, they "left the place marked by many cast off garments and the old faded Gray coat or jacket took the place of the blue Blouse..." Although Archer's brigade may have looked like a "brand new Brigade from Boston so completely were they clothed in Yankee uniforms" when they began their march, Mockbee's admission that they ditched their blue uniforms in favor of their Confederate uniforms as they neared the battlefield indicates Hill's soldiers were aware of the dangers of friendly fire and that they could become victims of it if they marched onto the battlefield in blue uniforms. Additionally, ditching the blue blouses lessened the weight the men had to carry on their march.[43]

Confederate sources also clearly state that Hill's men marched onto the Antietam battlefield under Confederate battle flags and, in some cases and against regulations, other banners.[44] When General Lee saw Hill's troops approach the battlefield, he asked for the assistance of artillery lieutenant John Ramsay. "What troops are those?" Lee asked. "They are flying the United States flag," Ramsay yelled as he looked in the direction of the Federal assault. Then, as Ramsay recalled, "General Lee pointed at another body of troops, nearly at right angles from the others" and moving from a different direction. "What troops are those?" Lee again inquired. "They are flying the Virginia and Confederate flags," replied Ramsay. "It is A.P. Hill, from Harper's Ferry," sighed a relieved Lee.[45]

Ramsay's account is important in establishing two crucial pieces of

---

43 Mockbee, "The 14th Tennessee Infantry Regiment," 21.

44 It is noted above that other Confederate regiments at Antietam carried two flags into battle, such as the 3rd North Carolina Infantry.

45 John A. Ramsay, "Tenth Regiment, Light Batteries, A, D, F, and I," in Clark, ed., *Histories*, vol. 1, 575. It is important to write that the only brigade of A.P. Hill's division that contained Virginia troops was Field's brigade, the last of Hill's brigades to reach the battlefield. At least one historian has notably speculated that the state flags Lee saw were actually South Carolina flags belonging to Maxcy Gregg's brigade, the division's vanguard. This would make sense considering the evidence presented hereafter. See Ethan S. Rafuse, *Antietam, South Mountain, and Harpers Ferry: A Battlefield Guide* (Lincoln, NE: University of Nebraska Press, 2008), 110.

evidence related to the flags Hill's men carried into battle. First, Ramsay, like Mockbee, specifically mention Hill's men fighting under Confederate flags. Ramsay's account also clearly differentiates between soldiers carrying the United States flag and the Confederate flag. Additionally, Ramsay confirms that despite army regulations which stipulated infantry units only carried one flag into battle, some of Hill's men carried two flags on September 17, which may have factored into Federal perceptions that they were being deceived by Stars and Stripes wielding Confederates.

Flag of the Pee Dee Artillery
(South Carolina Confederate Relic Room)

In 1861, United States Army regulations dictated that infantry regiments "were to carry two silk flags, each nearly six feet square: a national flag [the Stars and Stripes] and a regimental flag."[46] Federal soldiers seeing troops marching towards them carrying two flags into battle added to the confusion created by the setting sun, battle smoke, and tall corn. They likely thought that these were friendly troops advancing towards them, not the enemy. Also, though Union accounts designate the Stars and Stripes, predominantly blue flags may have been the cause of confusion in the swirl of battle in the Sherrick cornfield. Many of the Federal regimental flags featured a blue field. At least one of Gregg's regiments—the 1st South Carolina—that advanced into the cornfield flew its Palmetto flag with a blue field at Antietam.[47] Additionally, the first of A.P. Hill's troops to arrive on the battlefield, Capt. David G. McIntosh's Pee Dee Artillery, fought under a flag "made after the design of the State flag, a blue field

46 *Echoes of Glory: Arms and Equipment of the Union* (Alexandria, VA: Time-Life Books, 1996), 242-43.
47 Dedmondt, *Flags*, 46.

with the palmetto tree and crescent" with the words "Under This Standard We Will Conquer" emblazoned on it.[48] Despite army regulations, some of Hill's men did fly two flags in the Battle of Antietam, one of which was most certainly the Confederate battle flag.

From a distance and with the aid of a telescope, Ramsay was not the only one who easily saw the difference between Hill's troops and the Ninth Corps' soldiers. Lieutenant Joseph Gloskoski served as a signal officer atop Red Hill overlooking the Antietam battlefield. "From there we had full view of the enemy's lines," he reported. "We have reported immediately the positions and each change of position of all their batteries and their forces." By the afternoon of September 17, Gloskoski had been looking at the enemy lines for about two days. At 3 p.m. during the battle, he spotted another enemy movement and reported this to Maj. Gen. Ambrose Burnside, who commanded the Federals on the south end of the battlefield. "Look out well on your left; the enemy are moving a strong force in that direction." In his report, Gloskoski noted that this enemy was A.P. Hill's division.[49]

Confusion, terrain, terror, and battle smoke hindered the Federals' perception in the Sherrick cornfield on September 17, 1862. Their perception became their reality, and in the immediate aftermath of the Battle of Antietam, the tale floated that Confederates had played a dirty trick, a purposeful ruse to gain an advantage over their enemy. Prior experiences and social pressures made this ruse on the field of battle unlikely. Most of the Federal flags captured at Harpers Ferry by Hill's men were not actually captured but managed to evade Confederate troops. Those that did were smaller guidons or company flags, not the six square foot banners that Union troops carried into battle according to regulation. The soldiers of Hill's division did capture and wear Union uniforms but, once battle seemed imminent, traded them for their old gray uniforms in order to avoid confusion on the battlefield, not create it. From further vantage points, two separate officers—Ramsay and Gloskoski—had no trouble designating who was who. In the heat of the moment, in the swirling chaos of battle amidst smoke, waning daylight, rolling terrain, and head-high cornstalks, Union soldiers claimed to be deceived, but no Confederate sources support this deception. This myth of the Battle of Antietam, like the blue coats A.P. Hill's men left along

---

48 Mattie M. Brunson, "The Flag of the Pee Dee Battery," *Confederate Veteran,* March 1926, 94-95.
49 *OR,* vol. 19, pt. 1, 137-38.

the roadside on their way to Antietam, should be discarded from the history of the battle.

Very Much Diminished: Straggling in the Army of Northern Virginia in the Maryland Campaign
by Russell Rich

From the time it crossed the Potomac River into Maryland in the first week of September 1862 to the morning of the Battle of Antietam on September 17, 1862, Gen. Robert E. Lee's Army of Northern Virginia suffered an extensive amount of non-combat attrition. To the author's knowledge, no single article or paper to date has determined what effect, if any, that attrition had on the battle. This is surprising because this non-combat attrition, known at the time as straggling, resulted in tens of thousands of Lee's soldiers falling behind and not being physically present with the army at Antietam.[50]

The number of troops that Lee had on September 1, 1862, on the eve of his invasion of Maryland, is generally well-established based on "returns" or estimates done by Lee's officers of the strength of their units.[51] Based on these estimates, historians have concluded that Lee's effective strength at the beginning of September 1862 was approximately 65,000-70,000 men.[52] A mere two weeks later, by the morning of September 17, 1862, the army numbered only about 37,000 soldiers.[53] Confederate combat casualties during those two weeks were between 2,650 and 3,500.[54] Thus, the vast majority of Confederate attrition up to

---

50 Joseph L. Harsh, *Taken at the Flood: Robert E. Lee and Confederate Strategy in the Maryland Campaign of 1862* (Kent, Ohio: The Kent State University Press, 1999), 39. Harsh estimates Lee's strength on September 1 at 75,500. Bradley M. Gottfried, *The Maps of Antietam: An Atlas of the Antietam (Sharpsburg) Campaign, Including the Battle of South Mountain, September 2-20, 1862* (El Dorado Hills, CA: Savas Beatie, 2013), 4. Gottfried gives Lee's strength just before entering Maryland as "more than 70,000." Ezra A. Carman, *The Maryland Campaign of September 1862,* Thomas G. Clemens, ed., (El Dorado Hills, CA: Savas Beatie, 2012), vol. 2, 45. Carman, arguably the foremost authority on the battle, states total Confed. strength at Antietam as 37,351. Lee's strength therefore fell by 30,000 men in a little more than two weeks.
51 Harsh, *Taken at the Flood*, 39.
52 Ibid., 39; Gottfried, *Maps of Antietam*, 4.
53 Carman, *The Maryland Campaign*, vol. 2, 45.
54 The National Park Service estimates Confederate casualties at the Battle of South Mountain, prior to Antietam, were approximately 2,300. National Park Service, "Battle Detail: South Mountain." https://www.nps.gov/civilwar/search-battles-detail.htm?battleCode=md002. Accessed July 3, 2022. Joseph L. Harsh, *Sounding the Shallows: A Confederate Companion for the Maryland Campaign of 1862* (Kent, Ohio, & London, United Kingdom: The Kent State University Press, 2000), 222.

Antietam, possibly as many as 30,000 men, appears to have come from straggling. Even Maj. Gen. James Longstreet, who contended that the Army of Northern Virginia began the Maryland Campaign with only 57,000 infantrymen, estimated that "Lee lost nearly 20,000 [soldiers] by straggling..."[55] This leads one to wonder what caused Lee's army to lose anywhere from one-third to nearly one-half of its soldiers during those critical two weeks, perhaps the most important two weeks in American history.

To understand the phenomenon of straggling, we will examine it from Lee's own vantage point at the top, from the accounts of his generals who witnessed straggling winnow away their commands, and from the point of view of ordinary Confederate soldiers who directly experienced the hunger, exhaustion, lack of shoes, and sickness that caused so many men to fall behind the army. Many of these soldiers who fell out and became separated from Lee's army during the campaign appear to have rejoined it a few days or weeks after Antietam.[56] In this sense, the attrition experienced in Maryland was temporary, but all that attrition, clearly apparent in the thinned Confederate ranks on the morning of September

---

Harsh estimates total Confederate casualties at Harpers Ferry to have been 288, and 63 at Boonsboro on September 15, so adding those totals to the National Park Service's fairly conservative estimate of combat casualties at South Mountain would yield 2,651 total combat casualties during the campaign. Joseph Harsh and South Mountain historian John Hoptak believe Confederate casualties at South Mountain were actually higher. Harsh estimates Confederate casualties at 1,923 at Turner's Gap and 962 at Crampton's Gap. John David Hoptak, *The Battle of South Mountain* (Charleston, SC: The History Press, 2011), 61, 81, 106-108, 117, 121, 129. Hoptak gives fairly precise casualty figures for the various Confederate brigades engaged at Turner's and Fox's Gaps and totaling those figures together yields a casualty total for these two gaps at 2,192. Hoptak says "Confederate casualties [at Crampton's Gap] neared 1,000 men..." (163). Adding Harsh's more precise estimate of 962 Confederate casualties at Crampton's Gap to Hoptak's totals for the two northern gaps gives a Confederate total for South Mountain of 3,154. Adding to this the 288 Confederate casualties, estimated by Harsh, at Harpers Ferry, and 63 casualties at Boonsboro on September 15, puts combined Confederate combat casualties prior to Antietam at 3,505.

55 James Longstreet, "The Invasion of Maryland," in *Battles and Leaders of the Civil War* (New York: The Century Co., 1887), vol. 2, 674.

56 Darrell L. Collins, *The Army of Northern Virginia: Organization, Strength, Casualties, 1861-1865* (Jefferson, NC: McFarland & Company, Inc., 2016), 154-157. Collins' tables of the Army of Nothern Virginia's present for duty reports show Lee's total effective strength increased to 52,189 by September 30, 1862, only 13 days after Antietam. Collins' tables show Lee's effective strength grew further to 64,273 by Oct. 10, and up to 68,033 by Oct. 20, just over a month after Antietam.

17 meant that Lee would have too little strength at Antietam to seize the initiative the way he had done in earlier battles and he would do again in later ones. Nonetheless, the weakened units in the Army of Northern Virginia maintained their combat effectiveness.

Lee summarized the impact straggling had on his army during the campaign in a letter to President Jefferson Davis on September 23, 1862:

General Robert E. Lee (Library of Congress)

"The usual casualties of battle have diminished its [the army's] ranks, but its numbers have been *greatly* decreased [emphasis added] by desertion and straggling."[57] He told Davis that desertion and straggling "was the main cause of [the army's] retiring from Maryland, as it was unable to cope with advantage with the numerous host of the enemy."[58] Despite Lee's statement, straggling was not the reason that his army was forced out of Maryland.

According to Lee, Confederate straggling began while his army was still in northern Virginia before it crossed the Potomac into Maryland. He wrote a letter to Davis in which he said, "[a] great many men belonging to the army never entered Maryland at all..."[59] Major General Lafayette McLaws, one of Lee's division commanders, described some of this early straggling in a letter dated September 4,

---

57 *War of the Rebellion: The Official Records of the Union and Confederate Armies* (Washington, DC: GPO, 1887), Series 1, vol. 19, pt. 2, 622. Hereafter cited as *OR*, all citations from Series 1 unless otherwise stated.
58 Ibid.
59 *OR*, vol. 19, pt. 1, 143.

1862, shortly before McLaws' troops crossed the Potomac into Maryland:

> Riding off the road anywhere you can see parties of two & three & more settled in fence corners with green corn piled around & perhaps evidence of a meal from a stray hog or chicken. These men say they intend to join their regiment so soon as they become rested a little. They do not belong to any particular Corps but *to all Corps and divisions.* [emphasis added][60]

McLaws identified two factors that led to straggling: lack of food and lack of shoes. According to McLaws, over the course of three days at the beginning of September, his men had eaten meat one day, had only eaten "green corn" on another, and one day they had no food at all. The hunger that these men felt as they marched toward the Potomac River seems to have been a common experience in much of Lee's army. A Confederate soldier in Jackson's command said that his unit was not able to cook any rations at all between August 25 and September 4.[61]

Major General Daniel Harvey Hill echoed McLaws' complaints but also blamed fatigue and certain officers for the straggling. Hill said his men "had marched all the way from Richmond, and the straggling had been enormous in consequence of heavy marches, deficient commissariat, want of shoes, and inefficient officers."[62] McLaws summed up how many Confederate soldiers dealt with hunger, lack of shoes, and fatigue during the Maryland Campaign: "our men do not grumble, they only straggle."[63]

One Confederate soldier who straggled in northern Virginia was 19-year-old Cpl. Berry Benson of the 1st South Carolina Infantry.[64] Benson

---

60 Lafayette McLaws, *A Soldier's General: The Civil War Letters of Major General Lafayette McLaws,* John C. Oeffinger, ed., (Chapel Hill, NC: The University of North Carolina Press: 2002), 154-155.
61 John H. Worsham, *One of Jackson's Foot Cavalry: His Experience and What He Saw During the War 1861-1865* (New York: The Neale Publishing Company, 1912), 137.
62 *OR*, vol. 19, pt. 1, 1,021-22.
63 McLaws, *A Soldier's General*, 155.
64 Berry Benson, *Berry Benson's Civil War Book: Memoirs of a Confederate Scout and Sharpshooter*, Susan Williams Benson, ed., (Athens, GA: The University of Georgia Press, 2007), 24-25.

appears to have been one of the many soldiers in Lee's army who straggled due to illness. Benson recalled:

> We continued the march, moving toward Leesburg. I became more and more weak, marching out of ranks nearly all the time...The day after the army reached Leesburg (Sept 4) I was nearly played out, my Capt. begging me to stop and stay at some farm house till I got well. I answered no...I was out of ranks all day. Eating so little, I was very feeble...Next morning, Sept. 5, 1862, I fell in with the rest, but had to drop out before going twenty yards.[65]

Benson then became separated from his unit due to his illness, but caught up with it in time to fight at Antietam.[66]

Apart from men who were sick like Berry Benson, many of Lee's soldiers straggled during the Maryland Campaign due to hunger. Joseph Harsh, one of the foremost historians of the campaign, argues that at the beginning of September 1862, Lee's army faced a precarious food situation in northern Virginia. According to Harsh, although Lee had won the Battle of Second Manassas and forced the Union army to retreat to its defenses around Washington, the army "could not long remain in Fairfax County [Virginia]. The region had been picked clean of food and forage by the continuous fifteen months of occupation by the armies of both sides... Nor could Lee hope to freight in enough supplies...the railroad bridges over the Rapidan, the Rappahannock, and the Bull Run had been destroyed."[67] Lee's decision to invade Maryland was primarily a strategic one: he wanted to draw out and defeat the Union army, which he believed to be "weakened and demoralized."[68] However, one of Lee's top concerns during the Maryland Campaign was feeding his soldiers, and he made clear in his dispatches to President Davis that he intended to feed his troops locally from the countryside, first in Loudoun County, Virginia, and then in Maryland.[69] Despite Lee's efforts to find food for his soldiers, Confederate straggling due to hunger was a recurring problem during the Maryland Campaign.

---

65 Ibid., 25.
66 Ibid., xvi – xvii, 25-27.
67 Harsh, *Taken at the Flood*, 21-22.
68 Ibid., 57.
69 Ibid., 59

Separate from the issue of food, Lee's soldiers had another problem that caused many of them to straggle: a lack of shoes. Lee admitted to Davis before his army had even crossed the Potomac that "the men...in thousands of instances are destitute of shoes."[70] His decision to invade Maryland meant that thousands would be marching long distances barefoot. A Confederate soldier who experienced this hardship firsthand described it: "I had no shoes. I tried it barefoot, but somehow my feet wouldn't callous. They just kept bleeding. I found it so hard to keep up that though I had the heart of a patriot, I began to feel I didn't have patriotic feet."[71]

Another very committed Confederate soldier who experienced this problem was Color Sgt. George Branard of the 1st Texas Infantry. One source says that "[d]ue to many miles of marching with the Lone Star Flag, [Branard's] feet became bloody and sore. Major Matt Dale who saw his bare feet ordered Branard to the hospital, thus he missed fighting at Antietam."[72] Branard's unit went on to suffer 82% casualties at Antietam.[73] Had Branard been there, as color sergeant, his job would have been to carry his unit's state flag. This proved a particularly deadly task at Antietam, where one Texan said, "Eight men were killed and wounded...trying to bring [the state flag] off the field."[74] It is unclear if George Branard was ordered to the rear in Virginia, or in Maryland, but, in any case, his lack of shoes led him to miss serving at Antietam, and this quite possibly saved his life.[75]

Nor was George Branard's lack of shoes an isolated case. A veteran of the 4th Texas said in his account of the Battle of Antietam, "Many of us were barefooted and ragged."[76] The experience of Capt. William Plane from Georgia, showed that officers were not immune. "My feet are blistered top and bottom & my boots nearly entirely gone," he said. "One

---

70 Ibid., 60.

71 James V. Murfin, *The Gleam of Bayonets: The Battle of Antietam and the Maryland Campaign of 1862*, (Baton Rouge, LA: Louisiana State University Press, 1965) 95.

72 Joe Owen, Philip McBride, and Joe Allport, *Texans at Antietam: A Terrible Clash of Arms, September 16-17, 1862*, (England, U.K.: Fonthill Media Limited & Fonthill Media LLC, 2017), 57.

73 Ibid., 37-38.

74 Ibid., 68.

75 Ibid., 57, 60.

76 W.R. Hamby, "Hood's Texas Brigade at Sharpsburg," *Confederate Veteran*, vol. 16, 19.

more day's tramp & I shall be in the condition of hundreds in our army—barefoot."[77] In addition, McLaws had noted even before crossing the Potomac into Maryland that many of his men lacked shoes.[78] Later in the campaign, Lee himself supposedly remarked to one of his officers about how many soldiers in a North Carolina regiment had no shoes.[79] The number of soldiers who were marching barefoot in Maryland was by Lee's own estimate in the thousands and seems to have been a problem throughout the army.

There is also evidence that some Confederate soldiers who did not have proper shoes were either allowed to remain in rear-areas or lingered there on their own accord. David E. Johnston, who served in the 7th Virginia Infantry, asserted that at "Leesburg an order came for all sick and shoeless men to remain there."[80] Johnston's unit was part of Longstreet's command, and Lt. Alex Erwin from Georgia claimed that the order for shoeless men to stay at Leesburg came from Longstreet.[81] Lieutenant Erwin himself was unable to march due to blisters on his feet, and Erwin was put in charge of some of the "barefooted, weak and inefficient" men from his unit who were left behind in Leesburg.[82] A different soldier from Georgia also said, "Many of our men did not cross the river for want of shoes," though the soldier added that not all shoeless men stayed behind.[83] Surprisingly, Johnston said that the supposed order for the sick and barefoot to stay at Leesburg "was construed by a great many of the men to mean just anyone who did not want to go over the river into Maryland."[84] Johnston wrote "much too large a number of men remained at Leesburg, stretching the pretext to cover far more than was intended by the order."[85] Johnston himself had no shoes, but he chose to stay with the army and continue on into Maryland.[86] He estimated the

---

77 S. Joseph Lewis, Jr., ed., "Letters of William Fisher Plane, C.S.A. to His Wife," *The Georgia Historical Quarterly*, vol. 48, no. 2 (Georgia Historical Society, 1964), 224-25.
78 McLaws, *A Soldier's General*, 154.
79 Harsh, *Taken at the Flood*, 322.
80 David E. Johnston, *The Story of a Confederate Boy in the Civil* War, (Portland, OR: Glass & Prudhomme Company, 1914), 131.
81 D. Scott Hartwig, *To Antietam Creek: The Maryland Campaign of September 1862* (Baltimore, MD: The Johns Hopkins University Press, 2012), 97.
82 Ibid.; *The Southern Watchman* (Athens, GA), October 1, 1862.
83 Joseph T. Glatthaar, *General Lee's Army: From Victory to Collapse*, (New York, NY: Free Press, 2008), 167.
84 Johnston, *Confederate Boy*, 131.
85 Ibid.
86 Ibid., 133-134.

number of Confederate stragglers spread across a large swath of Virginia at about 20,000.[87]

One more possible cause of straggling in northern Virginia needs to be considered: soldiers temporarily leaving the ranks to visit family. The most striking account of this comes from Ezra Carman, a Union veteran of Antietam who, after the war, corresponded with many Union and Confederate veterans about their experiences during the Maryland Campaign. Carman recounts a frankly astonishing, though unverified, story of straggling in Garnett's brigade of D.R. Jones' division. Carman claimed a Confederate source in Garnett's brigade told him that while the brigade was in northern Virginia, two weeks before Antietam, "the men had been away from their homes for a very long time, and just left the ranks to see their old folks...wives and sweethearts, and did not rejoin until the army had recrossed into Virginia."[88] Although no other source corroborates this story of Garnett's men straggling to visit their families, it appears that over 70% of the men in Garnett's brigade did straggle for whatever reason.[89] Garnett's brigade numbered 1,739 men on September 2, 1862, but had less than 460 men in the ranks by the time of the Battle of South Mountain on September 14.[90]

Straggling in order to visit family did occur in the case of Solomon T. Blessing of the 1st Texas Infantry later on in the campaign. Blessing wrote, "When Gen. Lee crossed the Potomac into Maryland I was within ten or twelve miles of [my] mother's and sister's home in Brownsville [Maryland]. I took 'French leave' and as I knew the country well, went through the enemy's lines and visited my homefolks."[91] Blessing was only absent from the 1st Texas for a short time, and he rejoined his unit fairly easily.[92] However, any Confederate soldiers who left the ranks in Virginia for a week or more to visit their families would eventually have to take a

---

87 Ibid., 132.

88 Carman, *The Maryland Campaign*, vol. 2, 588.

89 Hartwig, *To Antietam Creek*, 679.

90 Ibid., 404, 679. Hartwig says Garnett had 407 men at South Mountain on pg. 404, but his table on pg. 679 shows their strength at 457.

91 Maimie Yeary, ed., *Reminiscences of the Boys in Gray 1861-1865*, (Dallas, TX: Smith & Lamar Publishing House M.E. Church, South, 1912), 60.

92 George E. Otott, "Clash in the Cornfield: The 1st Texas Volunteer Infantry in the Maryland Campaign," *Antietam: The Maryland Campaign of 1862: Essays on Union and Confederate Leadership, Civil War Regiments: A Journal of the American Civil War*, vol. 5, no. 3, Mark A. Snell, ed., (Campbell, CA: Savas Publishing Company, 1997), 77.

more roundabout route to rejoin the army. Lee issued an order on September 9 that stragglers still in Virginia should be diverted west to Winchester and only then sent north to join Lee in western Maryland.

Ezra Carman's story of family-related straggling in Garnett's brigade is also somewhat more conceivable when one considers that Confederate straggling was commonplace during the Maryland Campaign, and punishment for it seems to have been the exception rather than the rule. In a situation where straggling was treated laxly by officers, the desire to fall out briefly to visit nearby family, who one might not see again for many months, if ever, would be a powerful temptation.

For a variety of reasons, the straggling that Lee's army experienced in northern Virginia continued as it marched into Maryland. Alexander Hunter of the 17th Virginia painted an almost pitiful picture of sick, hungry, and barefoot infantrymen all around him as his unit marched through northern Virginia and then crossed the Potomac into Maryland:

> We were hungry, for six days not a morsel of bread or meat had gone in our stomachs—and our menu consisted of apples and corn. We toasted, we burned, we stewed, we boiled, we roasted these...until there was not a man whose form had not caved in, and who had not a bad attack of diarrhoea [sic]...half of the men were barefooted, many were lame and were sent to the rear; others...hobbled along and managed to keep up, while gangs from every company went off...looking for food, and did not rejoin their commands until weeks after. Many became ill from exposure and starvation, and were left on the road. The ambulances were full, and the whole route was marked with a sick, lame, limping lot.[93]

Hunter's account shows how the food that many Confederate soldiers consumed during the Maryland Campaign, mostly corn and apples, led to soldiers becoming sick with diarrhea and less physically able to keep up with the army. This reaffirms a recurring theme among Confederate sources that straggling resulted from several causes, including hunger, lack of shoes, and sickness. Hunter adds one more category of straggler: men "sent to the rear" due to being lame or physically unable to march.

Once Lee's army reached Frederick, Maryland, the physical condition

---

93 Alexander Hunter, "A High Private's Account of the Battle of Sharpsburg," *Southern Historical Society Papers*, vol. 10, 507.

and food supply of the soldiers seems to have improved, at least briefly. Lee wrote Davis on September 7 from Frederick: "I find there is plenty of provisions and forage in this country...I hope to procure subsistence for our troops."[94] One would think that after the army reached Frederick and rested there, some stragglers would have caught up with their now stationary units. Even so, Lee brought up the straggling issue to Davis. "One of the greatest evils, from which many minor ones proceed, is the habit of straggling from the ranks... With some, the sick and feeble, it results from necessity, but with the greater number from design." Lee seems to have shared Confederate soldier David Johnston's opinion that some Confederate stragglers did not have a legitimate excuse.

One Confederate soldier who straggled during this period with a slightly flimsy excuse was J.B. Polley from Texas. Polley admitted that he straggled briefly after crossing the Potomac because he wanted "to escape the heat and dust I should encounter if I remained in the ranks."[95] While straggling, Polley was lucky enough to acquire some meat from a butchered cow, which he then took with him to cook at his regimental mess.[96] Like Berry Benson who straggled due to sickness, and Solomon Blessing, who did so to visit family, Polley seems to have been committed to serving with his unit. He was briefly AWOL, but not a deserter. It also does not appear Polley was punished by his regiment for straggling, possibly because he was only absent from the ranks for a day or two.

By September 9, Lee's army was concentrated around Frederick, but that day Lee informed Davis that food in western Maryland was not as plentiful as he had hoped for:

> We are able to obtain forage for our animals and some provisions, but there is more difficulty about the *latter* [emphasis added]. Many of the farmers have not yet gotten out their wheat, and there is reluctance on the part of millers and others to commit themselves in our favor. I shall now open our communications with the valley, so that we can obtain more supplies. Some cattle, but not in any great numbers, are obtained in this country. The inhabitants are said to have driven many off to Pennsylvania.[97]

---

94 *OR*, vol. 19, pt. 2, 596.
95 J.B. Polley, *A Soldiers Letters to Charming Nellie*, (New York, NY and Washington, DC: The Neale Publishing Company, 1908), 80.
96 Ibid., 81.
97 *OR*, vol. 19, pt. 2, 602.

Lee reveals here that his army experienced two significant food supply problems in Frederick: insufficient local beef cattle, which his army could take with it and consume as it marched, and problems milling local wheat into flour to make bread. It seems that Lee had intended to mill the grain that his army acquired from the Maryland countryside in flour mills near Frederick. Abundant amounts of grain in Maryland would have been of little comfort if he could not mill that grain into flour. The "reluctance" of Maryland millers to cooperate with the Confederate army, combined with insufficient local beef cattle, seems to have been a major factor in Lee's decision to leave Frederick. He wrote on September 9, "I shall move in the direction I originally intended, toward Hagerstown and Chambersburg, for the purpose of opening our line of communication through the valley, *in order to procure sufficient supplies of flour* [emphasis added]."[98] The issue of an inadequate supply of food, that had already caused significant straggling from Lee's ranks in northern Virginia, continued to dog the army in Maryland.

On September 9, Lee issued Special Orders No. 191, in which he gave his army a detailed plan for the entire army to leave Frederick and march west and southwest towards Boonsboro and Harpers Ferry. Most of Lee's army would then surround or neutralize the large Union garrison at Harpers Ferry, which was in his rear and was a major threat to supply lines through the Shenandoah Valley. Lee's Special Orders No. 191 mostly dealt with marching orders for his troops, but it also dealt with certain stragglers. It instructed one of Lee's staff officers, Maj. Walter Taylor, to go to Leesburg, Virginia, which had been the main stopping off point on the Potomac River before crossing into Maryland, and "arrange for transportation of the sick and those unable to walk to Winchester...Those on the way to this army already across the river will move up promptly; all others will proceed to Winchester...being the general depot of the army."[99]

Lee's order seems to lend credence to Confederate soldier David Johnston's claim that there were a large number of Confederate stragglers at Leesburg, and that these men had not crossed the Potomac. Lieutenant Alex Erwin was one of the junior officers put in charge of the stragglers; he escorted the barefoot and otherwise unfit soldiers from his unit from

---

98 Ibid., 603.
99 Ibid.

Leesburg to Winchester.[100] Berry Benson also made that journey. He had straggled near Leesburg due to illness.[101] Benson recovered from his illness after five days, and attested to Confederate stragglers being sent to Winchester in compliance with Lee's order.[102] "Gen. Lee had issued orders that all stragglers repair to Winchester," he wrote, "as to attempt to follow on after the army in Maryland would result in almost certain capture."[103] Benson traveled to Winchester, then north to Harpers Ferry where he rejoined his unit.[104]

Confederates Marching through Frederick, Maryland, September 1862
(Historical Society of Frederick County, Maryland)

After Lee's army began to leave Frederick and carry out his plan, the commanding general accompanied one of his infantry columns west from Frederick to Hagerstown, Maryland. Lee then wrote another letter to

100 Hartwig, *To Antietam Creek*, 97; *The Southern Watchman* (Athens, GA), October 1, 1862.
101 Benson, *Civil War Book*, 25-26.
102 Ibid., 26.
103 Ibid.
104 Ibid., 26-27.

Davis describing the army's food situation. "We have found in this city about 1,500 barrels of flour, and I am led to hope that a supply can be gathered from the mills in the country, though I fear we shall have to haul from the Valley of Virginia," the general reported. "The supply of beef has been very small, and we have been able to procure no bacon."[105] This letter reiterates that local supplies of flour and meat in western Maryland were proving inadequate to feed the army. Lee's stated goal, early on in the campaign, "to supply ourselves with provisions and forage in the country in which we operate" had failed.[106] In the short term, this meant that many of the soldiers would continue to go hungry and might straggle from the ranks as a result.

Apart from the food supply issue, Lee had taken steps in Maryland to alleviate a different supply problem, the lack of shoes, by having the army purchase shoes in the towns it passed through. However, by September 12, his army had only been able to buy about 1,650 pairs of shoes in Frederick, Hagerstown, and in nearby Williamsport. Lee admitted these "will not be sufficient to cover the bare feet of the army."[107] Later, he contended that his quartermasters may have bought as many as 5,000 shoes while his army was in Maryland, but it "was by no means sufficient"[108] Much like Lee's soldiers' irregular supply of food, the lack of shoes continued to be an issue well into the Maryland Campaign.

On September 13, Lee gave President Davis an honest assessment of the cumulative effect that straggling had taken on the army up to that point. "One great embarrassment is the reduction of our ranks by straggling...Our ranks are very much diminished—I fear from a third to one-half of the original numbers—though I have reason to hope that our casualties in battles will not exceed 5,000 men." It is striking that Lee seemed to look for a silver lining in the fact that the 5,000 men he predicted losing in combat appeared to be less than the many thousands he had lost due to straggling.[109]

Though straggling was arguably more important to the attrition of Lee's strength during the Maryland Campaign, Confederate combat losses, particularly at the Battle of South Mountain on September 14, were significant and deserve consideration. As previously stated, on September

---

105 *OR*, vol. 19, pt. 2, 605.
106 Ibid., 594.
107 Ibid., 605.
108 Ibid., 614.
109 Ibid., 606.

9, Lee issued an order for his entire army to leave Frederick and move west. Then, from September 10 to 15, six of the nine divisions in his army endeavored to surround and capture Harpers Ferry. Although Lee tried to prevent straggling during this period, there is evidence that straggling continued.[110]

According to Mary Mitchell of Shepherdstown, Virginia, Confederate stragglers passed through her town on September 13.[111] Similar to earlier accounts of straggling, Mitchell said some stragglers had an excuse to be out of the ranks, and some did not. "They were stragglers...professional, some of them, but some worn out by the incessant strain of that summer. When I say that they were hungry, I convey no impression of the gaunt starvation that looked from their cavernous eyes."[112] Despite the straggling, Confederate forces under "Stonewall" Jackson, John Walker and Lafayette McLaws successfully surrounded Harpers Ferry, and on September 15, captured the town, its Union garrison, and a large amount of Union weaponry and supplies. The Confederates only suffered about 288 combat casualties while taking Harpers Ferry.[113]

While the majority of Lee's army was engaged in taking Harpers Ferry, two of his remaining three divisions traveled west to Hagerstown while the last remaining division under D.H. Hill stayed in the vicinity of South Mountain. Meanwhile, Maj. Gen. George B. McClellan's Army of the Potomac was approaching. When Union forces attacked D.H. Hill's troops at South Mountain on September 14, the two Confederate divisions at Hagerstown, under D.R. Jones and John Bell Hood, marched back to South Mountain and took part in the battle.

There appears to have been some straggling as these two Confederate divisions marched from Hagerstown back to South Mountain. Brigadier General Richard Garnett in Jones' division said his men marched eighteen miles to reach South Mountain that day and that the march to the battlefield was "hot, dusty, and fatiguing."[114] Colonel Joseph Walker,

---

110 Harsh, *Taken at the Flood*, 175.
111 Robert Krick, "The Army of Northern Virginia in September 1862: Its Circumstances, Its Opportunities, and Why It Should Not Have Been at Sharpsburg," *Antietam: Essays on the 1862 Maryland Campaign*, Gary W. Gallagher, ed., 42-43; Mary Bedinger Mitchell, "A Woman's Recollections of Antietam," in *Battles and Leaders of the Civil War* (New York: The Century Co., 1887), vol. 2, 687. Shepherdstown is now in West Virginia.
112 Mitchell, "Woman's Recollections," 687.
113 Harsh, *Sounding the Shallows*, 222.
114 *OR*, vol. 19, pt. 1, 894-97.

one of D.R. Jones' brigade commanders, stated that it was a "forced march."[115] Colonel F.W. McMaster of the 17th South Carolina described the march to South Mountain as "a most fatiguing march, under which some of our men broke down." David E. Johnston of the 7th Virginia remembered the "day was hot, the road hard and dusty, the march rapid— so much so that many of the men broke down, falling by the wayside."[116]

Campaign historian Scott Hartwig estimates that when D.R. Jones' division, Hood's division, and Evans' brigade arrived at South Mountain on September 14, their strength was significantly less than it had been on September 2.[117] Jones' division had decreased greatly from 9,034 men to 6,563, Hood from 3,839 to 2,970, and Evans from 1,058 to 550.[118] The most likely cause of this reduction in strength was straggling. It is difficult to determine exactly how much of the straggling occurred during the march from Hagerstown to South Mountain but since both David Johnston and F.W. McMaster, who were in entirely different brigades, mentioned straggling, the number of Confederate stragglers on September 14 appears to have been significant.

We will now consider the Confederate combat losses at the Battle of South Mountain to determine how significant they were compared to attrition due to straggling. Three Confederate infantry divisions and two infantry brigades from other divisions took part in the Battle of South Mountain. A detailed description of the fighting at South Mountain is beyond the scope of this essay. However, Confederate casualties at South Mountain need to be accounted for as one part of the general attrition of Lee's army during the Maryland Campaign.

Total Confederate casualties at Turner's and Fox's Gaps, two of the three South Mountain passes that were fought over in the battle, are estimated between 1,923 and 2,192.[119] In that fighting, D.H. Hill's division suffered approximately 1,031 combat casualties, and D.R. Jones' division suffered about 946 combat casualties. Evans' independent brigade, which was also at South Mountain, suffered about 215 casualties.[120] Hood's

---

115 Ibid., 905.

116 Johnston, *Confederate Boy*, 139.

117 Hartwig, *To Antietam Creek*, 679.

118 Ibid.

119 Harsh, *Sounding the Shallows*, 222.

120 Hoptak, *South Mountain*, 61, 81, 106-08, 117, 121, 129. Hoptak estimates the brigades of D.H. Hill's division suffered the following casualties: Garland—44 killed, 168 wounded, and "nearly 200 captured," G.B. Anderson—7 killed, 50 wounded, 30 captured, Rodes—61 killed, 157 wounded, 204 missing, and Colquitt—110 casualties.

division suffered only comparatively light casualties of 24 men.[121] There was also fighting at Crampton's Gap, which was the farthest south of the three passes through South Mountain that were contested. Confederate casualties at Crampton's Gap are estimated at 962.[122] The Confederate infantry that fought at Crampton's Gap were the brigades of Howell Cobb and William Mahone, the latter of which was headed by Lt. Col. William Parham.

The Army of the Potomac won a clear victory at South Mountain, capturing important passes through the ridgeline, arguably turning the tide in the Maryland Campaign, and taking the initiative away from Robert E. Lee. The night after the battle, Lee ordered his army to retreat from South Mountain so that his forces could reunite in Virginia. The next day, after learning that Harpers Ferry would likely fall to the Confederates that very day, Lee decided to reunite his entire army at Sharpsburg.

During the Confederate retreat from South Mountain to Sharpsburg, there appears to have been additional straggling from the Confederate ranks. D.R. Jones' division numbered 6,563 men at the Battle of South Mountain on September 14, and suffered 953 casualties there, but Jones' division had only 3,392 men in the ranks at Antietam on September 17.[123] It appears that 2,218 of Jones' soldiers straggled from the ranks during the Confederate retreat from South Mountain or have gone otherwise unaccounted for. Hood's division also decreased in strength. It numbered 2,970 at South Mountain, and suffered only 24 casualties there, but numbered 2,304 men at Antietam.[124] It appears that 642 of Hood's men straggled from the ranks during the retreat to Antietam. D.H. Hill's division likewise numbered 8,314 at South Mountain, and suffered 1,000 casualties there, but had only about 5,790 men in the ranks

---

Adding together Hoptak's estimates for D.H. Hill's four brigades yields a total of 1,031 casualties for Hill's division. Hoptak estimates the brigades of D.R. Jones' division suffered the following casualties: Drayton—206 killed, 227 wounded, 210 captured, Garnett—196 casualties out of 400 engaged, Kemper—75 casualties out of 400 engaged, Joseph Walker—32 casualties. Adding together Hoptak's estimates for Jones' brigades yields a total of 946 for Jones' division. Hoptak estimates Evans' casualties at 22 killed, 148 wounded, 45 captured, totaling 215.

121 Hartwig, *To Antietam Creek*, 679-80. Hartwig puts D.R. Jones' casualties at South Mountain at 953, Evans' at 216, and D.H. Hill's at 1,000.
122 Harsh, *Sounding the Shallows*, 222.
123 Hartwig, *To Antietam Creek*, 679.
124 Ibid.

at Antietam.[125] About 1,524 of D.H. Hill's men appear to have straggled between South Mountain and Antietam. For the divisions of D.R. Jones, D.H. Hill, and John Bell Hood, nearly half of all the straggling they experienced in the Maryland Campaign happened during the retreat from South Mountain to Antietam.[126]

We will next consider the significant straggling that occurred in the other two-thirds of Lee's army on September 16 and 17 as that part of the army marched approximately 17 miles from Harpers Ferry to Sharpsburg. Confederate straggling on the march appears to have been considerable. Six divisions made that march; we will first consider the three divisions under Stonewall Jackson's immediate command.

Brigadier General John R. Jones, whose division was part of Jackson's column, said that his troops left Harpers Ferry at 1 a.m. on September 16, crossed the Potomac after sunrise, and then reinforced Lee at Sharpsburg.[127] Brigadier General Jubal Early, a brigade commander in Jackson's column, recorded few details about the march from Harpers Ferry to Sharpsburg in his official report except to say that his men and another brigade were provided with rations prior to beginning their trek.[128] Like Jones' division, Lawton's division that Early's men belonged to crossed the Potomac shortly after dawn, and then joined Lee's army at Sharpsburg.

Despite neither Jones nor Early mentioning any straggling, there appears to have been about a 19% decrease in the strength of Jackson's three divisions between Harpers Ferry and Sharpsburg, which can only be explained by straggling. The National Park Service estimates Jackson's three divisions numbered approximately 14,000 men at Harpers Ferry.[129] However, Antietam veteran and historian Ezra Carman estimates that two of these divisions, under J.R. Jones and Alexander Lawton, numbered

125 Ibid., 680.
126 Ibid., 679-80. Per Hartwig, D.R. Jones' division lost 4,943 soldiers to straggling during the campaign. About 2,218 or 44.8% of these men left the ranks after South Mountain but before Antietam. Hood lost 642 of his 1,332 total stragglers during this time, or 48.1%. D.H. Hill lost 1,524 stragglers, or 49.8% of all his stragglers (3,057), during this time.
127 OR, vol. 19, pt. 2, 1,007.
128 Ibid., 967.
129 National Park Service, "1862 Battle of Harpers Ferry."
https://www.nps.gov/hafe/learn/historyculture/1862-battle-of-harpers-ferry.htm.
Accessed January 9, 2022.

only a combined 6,221 men on September 17, 1862.[130] The third division, under A.P. Hill, numbered perhaps 5,056 on the 17th.[131]

About 2,600 of Hill's men fought at Antietam, and another 1,000 were left behind at Harper's Ferry.[132] The remainder were present at Antietam but not really involved in heavy fighting, so their numbers were not well-recorded. Brigadier General James Archer was in A.P. Hill's division and described the journey from Harpers Ferry to Sharpsburg. "This was a long and fatiguing march; many of the men fell, exhausted...by the way, so that when the four regiments of my brigade reached the battle-field there were only 350 men."[133] It appears that Jackson's three divisions decreased in strength on the march to Antietam from about 14,000 men who were present at Harpers Ferry on September 16 to a little more than 11,277 still in the ranks the next day. This loss of about 19.45% of Jackson's combat soldiers was not insignificant.

One of the other Confederate divisions that made the march from Harpers Ferry to Sharpsburg was that of Lafayette McLaws. Unlike other Confederate troops who managed to get food from captured Union supplies at Harpers Ferry, McLaws said that many of his soldiers had no food prior to marching to Sharpsburg. McLaws' men also got little sleep two nights in a row. On the night of September 15, they crossed the Potomac River from Maryland to Harpers Ferry, and on the following night, September 16, they went back across the Potomac upstream at

---

130 Carman, *The Maryland Campaign*, vol. 2, 598. Carman puts Jackson's (J.R. Jones) division strength at Antietam as 2,094 including infantrymen and artillerymen. Carman puts Ewell's (Lawton's) division strength as 4,127. The two divisions combine to 6,221.

131 Ibid., 594, 598. Carman estimates A.P. Hill at 2,568 on September 17, but did not include Pender's, Field's (Brockenbrough's), or Thomas' brigades. Pender and Brockenbrough were present at Antietam but did not see much fighting. Dennis Frye estimates Thomas's strength at Harpers Ferry at approximately 1,000. Dennis, E. Frye, *Harpers Ferry Under Fire: A Border Town in the American Civil War* (Virginia Beach, VA: The Donning Company Publishers, 2012), 102. Carman, *The Maryland Campaign*, vol. 2, 598, estimated Branch, Gregg, and Archer had a combined 2,231 infantrymen on September 17. That averages to about 744 per brigade. If we use that same number for Pender and Brockenbrough, then they would have had a combined 1,488 men. Adding 1,488 to Carman's estimate for Hill's three most-active brigades (2,231), combined with artillerymen (337), and Frye's estimate for Thomas (1,000), would yield a total of 5,056 for the division on the 17th, between those in the ranks at Antietam and those with Thomas at Harpers Ferry.

132 Carman, *The Maryland Campaign*, vol. 2, 598; Frye, *Harpers Ferry Under Fire*, 102.

133 *OR*, vol. 19, pt. 2, 1,000.

Shepherdstown in order to get to Sharpsburg.[134] One of McLaws' officers, Brig. Gen. Joseph Kershaw, described the ordeal of his soldiers:

> ...my command were without their usual supply of subsistence from Monday morning, September 13, until the night of the 17th. They were also under arms or marching nearly the whole of the nights of Monday and Tuesday, arriving at Sharpsburg at daylight on Wednesday morning, September 17. As a consequence, many had become exhausted and fallen out on the way-side, and all were worn and jaded.[135]

W.B. Judkins from R.H. Anderson's division made the same march as McLaws' men and admitted to straggling because he was "broke down and worn out by so much hard marching."[136] McLaws' and Anderson's divisions combined may have numbered about 8,000 soldiers before setting out on the march from Harpers Ferry to Sharpsburg.[137] However, on the morning of the Battle of Antietam, these two divisions together numbered only about 6,961 men.[138] Apparently, a little less than 13% of McLaws' and Anderson's soldiers straggled on the march from Harpers Ferry to Sharpsburg.

The net result of six of Lee's divisions, two-thirds of his army, making the journey from Harpers Ferry to Sharpsburg was a large number of stragglers left behind on the route. A Confederate chaplain, Father James Sheeran, left a detailed account of the scene: "The country was literally crowded with stragglers. I presume that more than one half of [A.P.] Hill's Division had fallen out of the ranks during the march from Harpers Ferry to Shepherdstown, and I presume an equal proportion of the Divisions preceding it. Some of these men excited my sympathy, for they looked sick and broken-down but others again I looked upon with contempt, for they evidently were professional stragglers."[139] After Antietam, Father Sheeran was even more harsh, saying he personally blamed "the stragglers from our army" for "the prolonging of this

---

134 Ibid., 857.
135 Ibid., 864-65.
136 Hartwig, *To Antietam Creek*, 634.
137 Frye, *Harpers Ferry Under Fire*, 91; Hartwig, *To Antietam Creek*, 577.
138 Carman, *The Maryland Campaign*, vol. 2, 593. Carman put McLaws at 2,961 men on September 17 and R.H. Anderson at 4,000. Combined they would be 6,961.
139 James B. Sheeran, *Confederate Chaplain: A War Journal*, Joseph T. Durkin, ed., (Milwaukee, WI: The Bruce Publishing Company, 1960), 31.

barbarous war."[140]

It is clear that heavy Confederate straggling occurred in the run-up to the Battle of Antietam. However, Lee's two claims that desertion and straggling caused his forces to be "unable to cope with advantage with" the Union army, and that desertion and straggling were "the main cause" for his retreat back to Virginia were largely untrue.[141] This can be proven by considering the combat-performance at Antietam of the four divisions in Lee's army that experienced the highest straggling rates. These were the divisions of J.R. Jones, R.H. Anderson, D.R. Jones, and McLaws.[142]

Division	Strength on September 2	Strength on September 17	Non-Combat Attrition (primarily from straggling)
J.R. Jones	5,650[143]	2,094[144]	62.9%[145]
R.H. Anderson	11,024[146]	4,000[147]	62.1%[148]
D.R. Jones	9,034[149]	3,392[150]	51.9%[151]
Lafayette McLaws	7,759[152]	3,312[153]	44.9%

140 Ibid., 32.
141 *OR*, vol. 19, pt. 2, 622.
142 Hartwig, *To Antietam Creek*, 679-80. Hartwig estimates the straggling as 62% for J.R. Jones, 62% for R.H. Anderson, 55% for D.R. Jones, and 45% for McLaws.
143 Ibid., 679.
144 Carman, *The Maryland Campaign*, vol. 2, 598.
145 Hartwig estimates J.R. Jones' division's combat casualties at Harpers Ferry, its only combat operation between September 2-17, were 0. Hartwig, *To Antietam Creek*, 679.
146 Ibid.
147 Ibid.; Carman, *The Maryland Campaign*, vol. 2, 593.
148 Hartwig estimates R.H. Anderson's division's combat casualties between September 2-17 were 177. Hartwig, *To Antietam Creek*, 679.
149 Ibid.
150 Ibid.; Harsh, *Taken at the Flood*, 593.
151 Hartwig, *To Antietam Creek*, 679, says that Jones' straggling rate was 55%, but his numbers do not add up. Hartwig gives 9,034 for Jones on September 2, 953 casualties at South Mountain, and 3,392 present at Antietam. Those numbers yield a straggling rate of 51.9%.
152 Ibid., 680.
153 Ibid.

The other five division's in Lee's army, those of Alexander Lawton, John B. Hood, D.H. Hill, John Walker, and A.P. Hill all experienced straggling, but were nonetheless effective in combat at Antietam.[154] Although Hood, D.H. Hill, and most of Lawton's division were eventually defeated by Union forces, this was not due to straggling, but rather due to factors like terrain, massed Union infantry and artillery fire, the arrival of Union reinforcements from the Twelfth Corps, and Union tactics. Walker's division also suffered straggling prior to Antietam, but its combat operations in the West Woods were largely successful, so straggling cannot be said to have made it ineffective against Union forces. A.P. Hill's division suffered almost twice as much straggling as Walker's, but it was highly effective in combat at Antietam, saving the Confederate right from collapse.[155] Hill's troops were helped by the fact that they

---

154 Carman, *The Maryland Campaign*, vol. 2, 598; Harsh, *Sounding the Shallows*, 139; Hartwig, *To Antietam Creek*, 679. Their straggling rates were 35.3%, 35%, 31%, and 22.5%, respectively. See Footnote 155 for a detailed calculation of A.P. Hill's straggling rate: 40.2%.

155 A.P. Hill's division contained six brigades, five of which were at Antietam. Harsh put Hill's six brigades' strength as 8,570 on September 2. Harsh, *Sounding the Shallows*, 139. Hill left one brigade, under Thomas, at Harpers Ferry, and marched north to Antietam with the other five. Carman estimates Hill had 2,231 infantry and 337 artillerymen at Antietam. Carman, *The Maryland Campaign*, vol. 2, 598. Carman's estimate did not include three of Hill's brigades: those of Pender, Field, and Thomas. Pender's and Field's brigades were present at Antietam, but were not heavily engaged. Carman specifically said his estimate of 2,568 men for Hill at Antietam did not include Pender's or Field's brigades: "Pender and Field's brigades were on the extreme right and not engaged...and are not to be included in the estimate of fighting strength of the division." Carman, *The Maryland Campaign*, vol. 2, 594. Dennis Frye estimates that Thomas' brigade, which was left at Harpers Ferry, numbered about 1,000 men. Frye, *Harpers Ferry Under Fire*, 102. If we take 2,231 infantry (Carman's estimate for the total strength of the three brigades in Hill's division that were heavily engaged at Antietam) and divide by three, and use that number (743) as a baseline for Field and Pender, A.P. Hill had about 5,055 men present for duty at Antietam and Harpers Ferry on September 17. Hartwig estimates Hill's division suffered only 69 casualties at Harpers Ferry. Hartwig, *To Antietam Creek*, 679. It appears Hill's decrease in strength from 8,570 on September 2 to 5,055 on September 17, was almost entirely due to straggling. If we take the September 2 present for duty number (8,580), subtract 69 combat casualties, and 5,055 present on September 17, that means about 3,446 straggled from Hill's division, or 40.2% of Hill's September 2 strength. Hartwig estimates Hill's straggling was even higher at 64%, but Hartwig's total strength for Hill on September 17 of 3,014 seems too low. Hartwig, *To Antietam Creek*, 679. Out of Carman's estimate of 2,231 infantrymen for Gregg, Archer, and Branch, 750 were in Gregg's brigade. Carman, *The Maryland Campaign*, vol. 2, 464. James Archer stated in his report that his brigade numbered approximately 350 at Antietam. *OR,*

arrived relatively late in the day at an ideal tactical position—the Union left flank—and they also had good combat leadership. We will now consider the combat performance of the four Confederate divisions that experienced the highest straggling rates in the leadup to Antietam, the divisions of J.R. Jones, R.H. Anderson, D.R. Jones, and McLaws.

John R. Jones' division was driven back by Union forces during the battle, but this had more to do with effective Union tactics than with insufficient Confederate numbers from straggling. Jones' division numbered approximately 2,094 infantrymen and artillerymen on September 17, 1862, much smaller than the 5,650 men present for duty on Sept. 2.[156] The division suffered minimal combat casualties at Harpers Ferry, its only combat operation during those two weeks, so the straggling rate was approximately 62.9%.[157] Despite this straggling, Jones' division fought tenaciously at Antietam. After elements of the Union First Corps attacked Jones' line, Jones' men, by that time led by Brig. Gen. William Starke, counterattacked to briefly flank Union forces advancing through D.R. Miller's cornfield, but Starke's men were then themselves flanked by Union forces and driven back after intense fighting.[158] Union flanking tactics, not insufficient Confederate numbers resulting from straggling, were the main reason that Jones' division, later commanded by Starke, was driven back.

McLaws' division was paradoxically one of the most successful Confederate divisions at Antietam despite its non-combat attrition. As the Union army defeated Jones', Lawton's, and Hood's divisions and seized the East Woods and the Cornfield before advancing to the Dunker Church and West Woods, Lee deployed McLaws' division, numbering about 3,312, to prop up his embattled left.[159] McLaws' division had

vol. 19, pt. 1, 1,000. If we subtract 750 and 350 from 2,231, that leaves about 1,131 infantrymen in Branch's brigade. Hill also brought 337 artillerymen. Carman, *The Maryland Campaign*, vol. 2, 598. If we add Thomas' 1,000 men at Harpers Ferry as estimated by Frye to the 2,568 infantrymen and artillerymen at Antietam estimated by Carman, we have a total of 3,568, and Carman acknowledged that his estimate did not include Pender and Field. Therefore, Hartwig's estimate of 3,014 men in A.P. Hill's division on September 17 is too low.

156 Carman, *The Maryland Campaign*, vol. 2, 598; Harsh, *Sounding the Shallows*, 139. Hartwig estimates Jones' division at 5,578 on September 2. Hartwig, *To Antietam Creek*, 679.

157 Hartwig, *To Antietam Creek*, 679. Hartwig estimates J.R. Jones' casualties at Harper's Ferry were 0.

158 Carman, *The Maryland Campaign*, vol. 2, 75-79.

159 Hartwig, *To Antietam Creek*, 680. Carman estimates McLaws at 2,961. Carman,

numbered 7,759 men back on Sept. 2.[160] Although McLaws suffered some combat casualties at Crampton's Gap and Harpers Ferry, he lost close to 45% of his strength to straggling.[161] Nevertheless, McLaws' division was highly effective in combat at Antietam. It advanced to the West Woods and attacked the left flank of John Sedgwick's division of the Union Second Corps. Together with other Confederate units, McLaws' men drove back Sedgwick's Union troops in a matter of 20 minutes at the cost of 40% of Sedgwick's men. McLaws' division is a great example of Confederate troops at Antietam who suffered heavy straggling but were nonetheless effective in the battle because they had good combat leadership and a good tactical position from which they were able to flank Sedgwick's Union troops.

Although R.H. Anderson's division suffered heavy straggling before Antietam, and was defeated in the battle, this was largely due to Anderson being wounded, and a resulting lack of Confederate coordination, rather than due to thinned ranks. On September 2, 1862, the units that would later be combined together under Anderson numbered 11,024 men.[162] Fifteen days later, the same units numbered only 4,000 men.[163] The straggling in Anderson's division alone, about 6,847 soldiers, amounted to about 10% of Lee's September 2 strength.[164] Although R.H. Anderson's division suffered a straggling rate of 62.1%, the more important factor for it at Antietam was a loss of combat leadership. Anderson was wounded leading his division toward the Sunken Road. The division then became somewhat poorly coordinated. Union troops captured the Sunken Road and drove back Anderson's and D.H. Hill's divisions to the area of the Piper farm. The Union army captured both the Sunken Road and Burnside Bridge at approximately 1:00 p.m. McLaws' and Anderson's divisions both experienced heavy straggling

---

The Maryland Campaign, vol. 2, 598.

160 Hartwig, *To Antietam Creek*, 680. Harsh estimated McLaws slightly lower at 7,652 on September 2. Harsh, *Sounding the Shallows*, 139.

161 Hartwig, *To Antietam Creek*, 680. Hartwig lists 3,524 stragglers for McLaws or 45.4%, but if we deduct McLaws' 962 combat casualties from his September 2 strength (7,759 men), then it appears McLaws' stragglers actually totaled 3,485 men or 44.9%.

162 Hartwig, *To Antietam Creek*, 679.

163 Carman, *The Maryland Campaign*, vol. 2, 593.

164 Hartwig, *To Antietam Creek*, 679. According to Hartwig, Mahone's brigade in Anderson's division suffered 177 combat casualties at Crampton's Gap. Those appear to be all of Anderson's combat casualties between September 2 and the morning of September 17.

prior to Antietam. Despite this similarity, the two divisions performed very differently in combat at Antietam. For both McLaws' and Anderson's men, combat leadership and tactics, not straggling, made the difference between victory and defeat.

Lee was perhaps closest to being correct in the case of D.R. Jones' over-stretched division, which was driven back south of Sharpsburg. When the Union Ninth Corps began its final attack on Sharpsburg at about 3:00 p.m., D.R. Jones' division was the only division Lee had on that part of the field to stand in the Ninth Corps' way. Jones' men were heavily outnumbered. The six brigades of Jones' division numbered 9,034 on September 2.[165] On September 17, these six brigades had only 3,392 men.[166] Allowing for combat-casualties at South Mountain, it appears that Jones lost about 51.9% of his men to straggling.[167]

The two units in the entire Confederate army that perhaps came closest to proving Lee's point were Garnett's and Kemper's brigades of Jones' division, which were driven back near the end of the battle. At the start of the campaign, Kemper and Garnett had a combined strength of 3,101.[168] Outside Sharpsburg, Garnett had only 261 men, and Kemper had 443, for a combined total of 704.[169] It appears 2,126 men, a staggering 68.5%, straggled from Kemper and Garnett's brigades by the Battle of Antietam.[170]

For Garnett and Kemper's brigades, Lee's assertion that straggling had

---

165 Ibid. The six brigades that D.R. Jones commanded at Antietam had been two separate divisions earlier in the campaign. Joseph Harsh lists D.R. Jones' three brigade division (Toombs, G.T. Anderson, and Drayton's brigades) at 3,728 men present for duty on September 2 and 4,887 present for duty in Kemper's division (Kemper, Jenkins, and Garnett) that same day. Harsh, *Sounding the Shallows*, 139. According to Hartwig, Jones' division suffered a total of 953 casualties at South Mountain. Hartwig, *To Antietam Creek*, 679. If we subtract the combat casualties and those present on September 17, we get a total of 4,270, or 49.5% of the division's September 2 strength as estimated by Harsh, who appear to have straggled.

166 Hartwig, *To Antietam Creek*, 679, says that Jones' straggling rate was 55%, but his numbers do not add up. Hartwig gives 9,034 for Jones on September 2, 953 casualties at South Mountain, and 3,392 present at Antietam. Those numbers yield a straggling rate of 51.9%.

167 Ibid., 680.

168 Ibid., 679. Kemper had approximately 1,362 men and Garnett had about 1,739.

169 Carman, *The Maryland Campaign*, vol. 2, 588; Hartwig, *To Antietam Creek*, 679.

170 Hoptak and Hartwig estimate that Kemper and Garnett combined suffered 271 casualties at South Mountain. Hoptak, *South Mountain*, 121; Hartwig, *To Antietam Creek*, 679. Subtracting 271 casualties and the 704 present on September 17 from the 3,101 September 2 strength yields 2,126 stragglers, or 68.5%.

rendered them unable to cope with Union forces was perhaps accurate as both were defeated. Another of Jones' brigades, Drayton's brigade, was also driven from its position, but it had taken over 43% casualties three days earlier at South Mountain and had suffered far less straggling on the march to Antietam, so straggling cannot be said to have made it combat ineffective.[171]

After Garnett, Kemper, and Drayton's brigades were defeated and driven into Sharpsburg, the Ninth Corps advanced tantalizingly close to the town. Lee's army only averted disaster because A.P. Hill's division arrived on the Union left flank, forcing the Federals to abandon its advance towards Sharpsburg and fall back towards Antietam Creek.

On the night of September 18, 1862, Lee's army returned to Virginia. The army's strength then rapidly increased in October 1862.[172] Colonel Edward Porter Alexander said that during this time "tens of thousands of stragglers left along the roadsides" returned to the army, and also "a good many fresh men from home came on."[173] According to Darrell Collins' tables in *The Army of Northern Virginia: Organization, Strength, Casualties: 1861-1865*, Lee's total effective strength increased to 52,189 by September 30, 1862, only 13 days after Antietam, grew further to 64,273 by October 10, and eventually to 68,033 by October 20. A return to the army's pre-Maryland Campaign strength did not make up for the fact that he had been forced out of Maryland and had not achieved his campaign goals. Instead, the Union army drove Lee out of Maryland and Abraham Lincoln used that Union strategic victory to issue the Emancipation Proclamation.

The straggling of between 20,000 to 30,000 of Lee's soldiers between September 2 and September 17, 1862, led his army to be seriously understrength at Antietam, and, to a certain extent, that robbed Lee of the tactical initiative he had seized in earlier battles on the Peninsula and at Second Manassas. Without the initiative, he could not win the kind of

---

171 Hartwig, *To Antietam Creek*, 679. Drayton's casualties at South Mountain were 43.9%. Hartwig lists Drayton's September 2 strength as 1,464, and states that the brigade took 643 combat casualties at South Mountain (43.9%) and had 465 men in the ranks at Antietam. Subtracting 643 and 465 from 1,464 gives the number of stragglers as 356, or 24.3%.
172 See Collins, *The Army of Northern Virginia*, 154-57, re. Lee's rapid increase in strength during October.
173 Edward Porter Alexander, *Fighting for the Confederacy: The Personal Recollections of General Edward Porter Alexander*, Gary W. Gallagher, ed. (Chapel Hill, NC: University of North Carolina Press, 1998), 155.

clear victory that he had in mind when he entered Maryland. However, it was not true, as Lee later claimed, that straggling was the reason the army was driven out of Maryland or that straggling caused Confederate troops at Antietam to be "unable to cope with advantage with the numerous host of the enemy."[174] Five Confederate divisions, those of Lawton, Hood, D.H. Hill, Walker, and A.P. Hill, experienced considerable straggling, but were nonetheless effective in combat at Antietam.[175] McLaws' division performed very well at Antietam despite even heavier straggling.[176] R.H. Anderson's division did poorly at Antietam, but largely because Anderson was wounded at a critical moment, not because of straggling. J.R. Jones' division also experienced heavy straggling, but performed well in combat up until the point it was flanked by Union troops.

Lee was perhaps most right in the case of D.R. Jones' division. Prior to the Battle of Antietam, Jones' division lost 4,689 of its soldiers, or 51.9% of its pre-campaign strength, to straggling.[177] Given that Col. Harrison Fairchild's brigade, the Union brigade that broke through two of D.R. Jones' brigades at Antietam, suffered one of the highest proportion of casualties of any Union brigade at Antietam, largely due to Confederate artillery fire, it is hard to believe such a bloody Union attack would have succeeded had Jones' stragglers been present. However, the Union's hard-won breakthrough against Jones' division came to nothing because of the arrival of A.P. Hill's division on the Union left flank. Thus, even where straggling arguably helped bring about a Union breakthrough at Antietam, other Confederate units that suffered heavy straggling forced Union troops to fall back. Therefore, Lee's statement to Davis that straggling was the "main cause" of the army being forced out of Maryland, was not accurate.

The main cause of Lee's army being driven out of Maryland was quite simply the Union army. At Antietam, it defeated three Confederate divisions near the Cornfield and two Confederate divisions at the Sunken Road, more than half of the nine infantry divisions in Lee's army. Straggling was not the reason for Confederate defeat in either part of the

---

174 Ibid.
175 Hartwig, *To Antietam Creek*, 679-80; Carman, *The Maryland Campaign*, vol. 2, 593, 598; Harsh, *Sounding the Shallows*, 139. Their straggling rates were 33.9%, 39.3%, 31%, and 23.4%, respectively. See Footnote 155 for a detailed calculation of A.P. Hill's straggling rate: 40.2%.
176 See Footnote 161 regarding McLaws' straggling rate, approximately 44.9%.
177 Hartwig, *To Antietam Creek*, 679.

battlefield. Far from that being the "main cause" of the Confederates' being driven out of Maryland, as Lee claimed, Confederate units' experience at Antietam showed that unit cohesion could endure very well despite straggling and that combat leadership, tactics, and a unit's position on the battlefield relative to the enemy were, for most units, much more important than straggling to determining battlefield success or failure.

In Their Own Words: The Lost Passages of Brig. Gen. Alfred Pleasonton's Report of the Battle of Antietam by Kevin R. Pawlak

The published pages of the *Official Records of the War of the Rebellion* make the process of writing correspondence and after-action reports appear to be a neat, straightforward process. The printed pages of the *Official Records* hide the ink splotches, strikethroughs, and edits necessary to reach a final draft. Their omissions obscure the process of writing and revisions that went into producing the valuable source material found for historians today in the *Official Records*.

Brigadier General Alfred Pleasonton
(Library of Congress)

Brigadier General Alfred Pleasonton's Maryland Campaign report was one such report. Pieces of his original draft ended up on the drawing room floor—or the floor of his tent—and never made it to print. Thankfully, they did survive and can be found in a box of Maj. Gen. George B. McClellan's Papers at the Library of Congress.

Pleasonton's original report was critical of Fifth Corps commander Fitz John Porter's actions during the Battle of Antietam. It remains unclear why Pleasonton changed to a softer tune about Porter in his final report, though historian William Marvel has speculated that Pleasonton "deleted [them] when McClellan apprised him of his mistaken assumptions about Porter and his command."[178] The report that made it into the Army of the Potomac's

178 William Marvel, *Radical Sacrifice: The Rise and Ruin of Fitz John Porter* (Chapel Hill, NC: University of North Carolina Press, 2021), 412-13, n. 43.

files can be found in Part 1, Volume 19, of the *Official Records* running between pages 208 and 213. Rather than presenting Pleasonton's entire report here, I have reproduced it as it appeared in the general's first draft. The non-italicized font highlights the sections that made it into Pleasonton's final report while the italicized font shows the sections that did not make the cut.

*   *   *   *   *   *   *   *   *   *

It was now 4 o'clock in the afternoon. Burnside's corps had driven the enemy back upon the hill upon which his batteries were placed, and, in conjunction with the repulse of the enemy in front of Hancock, left the field open to the Sharpsburg Ridge, to which point I desired to forward my batteries, to obtain an enfilading fire upon the enemy in front of Burnside, and enable Sumner to advance to Sharpsburg. I was so satisfied that this could be done at that moment, that I sent a request to Major General Fitz John Porter, asking for the assistance of some infantry to support my advance to the Sharpsburg Ridge.

I was advised to "exercise caution so as not unnecessarily expose my batteries;" and further, "that the cornfield on my left is full of rebel infantry;" and "the ridge at Sharpsburg is lined with the enemy's infantry." General Porter was at least one mile and a half to the rear of my position when he sent me this advice & information, and he had not been to the front or on the Sharpsburg side of the Antietam creek at any time during that day, so far as I have been able to ascertain. I knew he was ignorant of the state of affairs at that time, was my reason for sending my request to enlighten him; & I further knew that he was the only officer on that field at that moment who was in the situation to take advantage of the embarrassing condition of the enemy. Decisive victory which was then within our grasp was lost to us by this inaction & apathy; for the enemy finding that no advance was made from the center, massed his troops against Burnside, who was compelled to fall back on the Antietam creek.

I held my position until seven o'clock in the evening when I was withdrawn by the orders of Major General McClellan to the bivouac at Keedysville.

This request was not entertained by General Porter, and I have since been informed the force I needed was not then at his disposal. I held my position until 7 o'clock in the evening, when I was withdrawn, by the orders of Major-General McClellan, to the bivouac at Keedysville.[179]

179 *War of the Rebellion: The Official Records of the Union and Confederate Armies* (Washington, DC: GPO, 1887), Series 1, vol. 19, pt. 1, 212; Draft of

Antietam Artifacts: A Carte de Visite of Antietam Veteran Thomas E. Cutter, 35th Massachusetts Infantry
by Joseph Stahl

Twenty-six-year-old Thomas E. Cutter of the 35th Massachusetts Infantry was one of thousands of soldiers who served on the Antietam battlefield that brutal September 17th. Cutter was born on March 28, 1836, in Newburyport, Massachusetts. He was mustered into Co. B, 35th Massachusetts Infantry for three years on August 19, 1862, less than a month before the Battle of Antietam, giving up his job as a painter.[180]

Cutter mustered in as 3rd Corporal at Camp Stanton, Massachusetts, according to his service records. The roll for August 11 to October 31, 1862, shows he was "present" for the period and notes that Cutter was "detailed as Quarter-master clerk Aug. 26/62." His service records next note that he was promoted to sergeant on October 31, 1862. He was present in November and December 1862 and would continue to be during most of his service. Cutter was promoted again on January 1, 1863, to Quartermaster Sergeant, and then again on April 1, 1864, to 1st Lieutenant and Regimental Quartermaster. He requested a twenty day leave of absence to return home to resolve some issues with his business on January 9, 1865. When his term of service ended on June 9, 1865, he was mustered out in Alexandria, Virginia. The form noted that he had last been paid on December 31, 1864.[181] Cutter filed for a pension on July 16, 1902.[182] But he did not live long after that date. He passed away on May 26, 1903, and is buried in Oak Hill Cemetery in Newburyport, his home town.[183]

Cutter's picture was taken when he was a 1st Lieutenant. He is seated

---

Pleasonton's Report, Box A88, Reel 35, George Brinton McClellan Papers, Library of Congress.

180 "Thomas Cutter," Civil War Database, accessed on February 28, 2022, http://www.civilwardata.com/active/hdsquery.dll?SoldierHistory?U&77487.
181 Thomas Cutter Military Service Records, Company B, 35th Massachusetts Volunteer Infantry, National Archives and Records Administration.
182 Pension Card Index, National Archives and Records Administration, accessed February 28, 2022, https://www.fold3.com/image/2740368.
183 "Thomas Cutter", Find-a-Grave, accessed February 28,2022, https://www.findagrave.com/memorial/101118668/thomas-edwin-cutter.

and the back of the chair is visible. He wears a neat bow tie and a handkerchief in his coat pocket. His shoulder boards show the single bar of a 1st Lieutenant, and he is also wearing a vest. Written on the back is "Lt. Cutter R.Q.M. 35 Mass. Before Petersburg Va March 6/65". Although the photograph does not have a tax stamp on it, the photographer was "Batchelder & Clement, Photographic Artists, Essex Hall Building, 39 State Street, Newburyport, Mass." The photo was probably taken when he returned from his service.

At Antietam, Cutter's 35th Massachusetts served in Brig. Gen. Samuel Sturgis' division in the Ninth Corps. The regiment was organized at Camp Stanton, Lynnfield, and was composed mostly of men from eastern Massachusetts. It was recruited during July and early August 1862, with its members mustering into service between August 9 and 19. The regiment left for the front on August 22, reaching Washington two days later. On September 8, the 35th Massachusetts was assigned to Col. Edward Ferrero's brigade.[184]

After joining the Army of the Potomac, the regiment first saw combat in the Maryland Campaign, fighting at both South Mountain and Antietam. In both actions, the 35th Massachusetts sustained heavy losses. At Antietam, the regiment was under command of Maj. Sumner Carruth and had about 780 men under arms.[185]

The regiment reported 48 killed, 160 wounded, and 6 missing for a total of 214 casualties at Antietam.[186] Cutter's regiment likely suffered most of these causalities during the Final Attack where the regiment was heavily engaged. The regimental history describes the approach and crossing of the Burnside Bridge:

> Our regiment came partly into line, as if to open fire along the bank at the bridge; then, by the colonel's commands swung by the right again and joined the throng hurrying on to the further bank, the third regiment to cross... In a shorter time than it takes to tell it we had crowded across the bridge and filed into the road to the right, where the two regiments which had preceded us were halted... Men in gray came down the hill, holding up both hands,

184 The Adjunct General, *Massachusetts Soldiers, Sailors and Marines in the Civil War,* vol. 3 (Norwood, MA: The Norwood Press, 1932), 645.

185 Carman, *The Maryland Campaign,* vol. 2, 580.

186 John Michael Priest, *Antietam: The Soldier's Battle* (Shippensburg, PA: White Mane Publishing, 1990), 340.

or waving a dirty white rag, and were sent to the rear as prisoners. They belonged to Georgia regiments, of Toombs's Brigade, of General D. R. Jones's Division.[187]

The regiment then moved over a hill before withdrawing to avoid Confederate artillery fire. The regimental history notes:

> A shell, skimming the crest of the hill, stole a haversack from a man's back as he lay upon the ground, and sent it flying towards the stream below, exciting merriment in spite of the gravity of the situation. The whirring of the shells above us had a drowsing effect, and some of our men dozed; others munched hard bread and conversed in low tones; some went for water by detail, filling canteens from the warm, soft water of the creek. At such a time men's characters reveal themselves: the religiously disposed bends his thoughts on Heaven; the less devout watches the ants busy as usual at their never-ending labors, and wishes he could be as small as they for a few hours; while the more thoughtless cuts his tobacco and enjoys its soothing influence. We lay thus several hours while troops were coming over.[188]

Later when ordered forward, the regiment "charged with a hurrah, on the double quick over the hill from which the 9th New York had charged, and down the slope, passing some broken commands, to the rail fences of Otto's lane, where it halted in a very exposed position, laid its rifles on the fence rails and opened fire."[189]

Brigadier General Jacob Cox then sent the large regiment over the hill.

> We passed the remnants of the first line and kept on to a rail fence, partly broken down, enclosing a lane, into which some of the men climbed. Here we halted, and laying our rifles upon the rails. Opened fire at will upon the enemy coming on to follow up their success.

---

187 Committee of the Regimental Association, *History of the Thirty-Fifth Regiment Massachusetts Volunteers, 1862-1865,* (Boston, MA: Mills, Knight & Co., Printers, 1884), 41-42.
188 Ibid., 44-45.
189 Carman, *The Maryland Campaign,* vol. 2, 484.

In front was a ploughed field, sloping up to a wall of most solid construction, about two hundred yards off; on the left front. Cornfields with high stalks and waving blades uncut. Beyond these the hill rose more steeply to the summit, upon which were the enemy's batteries. Behind the wall and in the cornfield was the Confederate Infantry.

It was a steady roll of musketry. The officers directed the aim of the men, Captain Cheever's quaint phase being "Pop away! Boys, Pop away!"

Ammunition was failing us, and Captains Andrews (acting Lieutenant Colonel), King and Lathrop passed along the line, opening the boxes of the fallen and distributing the cartridges found.[190]

That evening, "Captain Lathrop and Lieutenant Hudson, receiving information of wounded men within reach from Corporal Whitman (for he and several men of Company G appear to have been the last fighting men to leave the rail fence), tried with a squad of men, to make their way in the intense darkness down to the fence to care for the wounded; but the party was stopped by a line of pickets from the Fifty-First Pennsylvania..." Corporal Frank M. Whitman was finally permitted to make the attempt and rescued a wounded comrade. He received a Medal of Honor for this action.[191]

The regiment suffered again severely at the Battle of Fredericksburg on December 13, 1862. It was fortunate to avoid the infamous Mud March and remained in winter quarters near Falmouth through the winter of 1863.[192]

The following spring, the 35th Massachusetts was sent with the Ninth Corps to Kentucky. Following the fighting in the Western Theater, the regiment returned to Cincinnati during the winter of 1864 and was ordered first to Baltimore, Maryland, before traveling to Annapolis. Still part of the Ninth Corps, the 35th Massachusetts was next engaged during the Overland Campaign in 1864. Following this action the regiment participated in the Siege of Petersburg, operating as engineers of the First

---

190 *History of the Thirty-Fifth Regiment Massachusetts Volunteers,* 46, 47, 49.
191 Ibid., 51.
192 Ibid., 99.

Division, Ninth Corps. In this role, the men were heavily engaged in the Battle of the Crater on July 30. Severely reduced by combat, the regiment was assigned to Fort Sedgwick, better remembered as Fort Hell, in March 1865, and remained there until the fall of Petersburg on April 2, 1865.

The 35th Massachusetts joined in the pursuit of the Army of Northern Virginia and was at Farmville, Virginia, when news of the surrender arrived. The regiment was ordered to Alexandria and remained as a part of the garrison of the District of Columbia until June 9, when it transferred its recruits to the 29th Massachusetts and its remaining men mustered out of service. On June 27, 1865, the 35th Massachusetts returned to Readville, Massachusetts, where the men were paid off and the regiment discharged.[193]

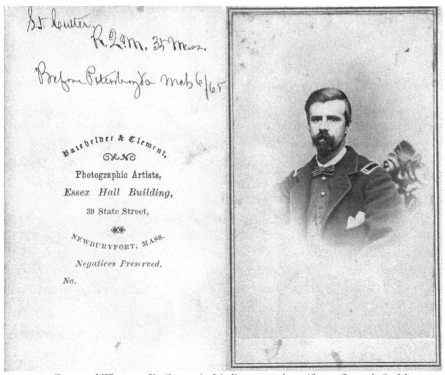

Corporal Thomas E. Cutter in his lieutenant's uniform (Joseph Stahl)

193 *Massachusetts Soldiers, Sailors and Marines in the Civil War*, vol. 3, 645-646.

In Antietam's Footsteps: Hiking the Crampton's Gap Loop Trail
by J.O. Smith

Late on the afternoon of September 14, 1862, Brig. Gen. Howell Cobb led his Confederate brigade toward Crampton's Gap with orders to "hold the gap if it cost the life of every man in [his] command." Threatening the gap was Maj. Gen. William B. Franklin's Sixth Corps of the Army of the Potomac, on the march to relieve the beleaguered Union garrison at Harpers Ferry. From the heights at the gap, the Confederate defenders had the advantage of a steep elevation the Federal troops would have to ascend to force the position. A new loop trail at the gap challenges visitors to experience that terrain, over which a running fight cost Cobb's brigade close to 700 men.[194]

The trail begins at the 1896 War Correspondents Memorial Arch and descends the eastern slope of South Mountain. A series of waysides describes the action on the late afternoon and evening of September 14. The fight for the gap began around 5:30 p.m. at the base of the mountain where a thin line of Virginians and Georgians formed to meet the oncoming Federals from behind a stone fence topped in certain spots by wooden rails along Mountain Church Road. By the time the action reached the area of the trail, the Confederate line along the road below had broken, with pursued and pursuer climbing the slope toward the gap. Amid the trees, the trail offers vistas of the rough ground that must have exhausted many a soldier that day. The regimental history of the 5th Maine Infantry put it this way: "Our position was a difficult one. There was the mountain in our front, steep and high, guarded by a heavy force of infantry, with a body of cavalry and a battery, and our division was expected to storm and take it. It looked almost impossible." Colonel Joseph Bartlett, whose brigade led the Federal assault, reported that "the appearance of the mountain pass convinced all that artillery was of no avail against it, and that nothing but a combined and vigorous charge of infantry would carry the mountain." If you proceed downhill to the right

---

194 United States War Department: *The War of the Rebellion: A Compilation of the Official Records of the Union and Confederate Armies* (Washington: U.S. Government Printing Office, 1880-1901), vol. 19, pt. 1, 870; Ezra Carman, *The Maryland Campaign of September 1862,* Thomas Clemens, ed., (El Dorado Hills: Savas Beatie, 2010), vol. 1, 312.

from the arch, you first come to a wayside providing an overview of the fight for the gap.[195]

Looking down the slope of South Mountain into the Middletown Valley. (J.O. Smith)

To your right as you descend the slope is Gapland Road running downhill toward Burkittsville, from which Franklin's troops launched their assault on the gap. Franklin described the road as making a "steep

---

195 George W. Bicknell, *History of the Fifth Regiment Maine Volunteers, comprising brief descriptions of its marches, engagements, and general services from the date of its muster in, June 24, 1861, to the time of its muster out, July 27, 1864* (Portland: H.L. Davis), 136; *OR*, vol. 19, pt. 1, 388.

ascent through a narrow defile, wooded on both sides, and offering great advantages of cover and position." Further down, you come to the Cobb's Georgia Legion wayside in the area where 248 Georgians under the command of Lt. Col. Jefferson Lamar tried to form a line in the face of advancing Union troops who had broken through the Confederate position at the Mountain Church Road. Lamar fell mortally wounded in this area. On every battlefield, the fates place certain units in a bad spot, and so it was for Lamar's troops. With little time for proper deployment, the Georgians took fire on their flank while trying to form. The Legion suffered a casualty rate of more than 70%. Along the trail, one might contemplate how they lost so heavily despite the seeming advantage of advancing downhill to face an enemy attacking up a steep slope. Colonel Thomas Munford, whose troopers were the initial Confederate defenders of the gap, blamed Cobb and his men, recounting that Cobb's brigade "behaved badly and did not get in position before the wildest confusion commenced, the wounded coming to the rear in numbers and more well men coming with them." In his after-action report, Cobb wrote that "we were flanked on both the right and the left by the enemy, and, thus surrounded, our men were compelled to surrender." A member of the Legion wrote to his wife after the battle, "I guess you have heard before now of the sad fate of Cobb's Legion. They were cut to pieces on Sunday the 14th. The Yankees flanked our men on the right & left." Bartlett suggested that attacking uphill worked to the Federals' advantage, the Confederates "firing over us" from above, while for the attackers firing uphill, "each bullet must hit either a tree, a rock or a man, for they could not go over the mountain."[196]

From the Legion's marker, the trail winds north to a wayside describing the fight in Whipp's Ravine, where the 24th Georgia of Cobb's brigade formed partway up the slope behind the position along the Mountain Church Road. Though the trail does not go all the way down to the road, the battlefield tramper can get a view through the trees (especially in the winter months) of the ground over which the Confederates retreated from the road pursued by Sixth Corps troops. The trail climbs back toward the

196 OR, vol. 19, pt. 1, 375, 827, 871; Bradley M. Gottfried, The Maps of Antietam: An Atlas of the Antietam (Sharpsburg) Campaign, Including the Battle of South Mountain, September 2-20, 1862 (El Dorado Hills: Savas Beatie, 2012, 2013), 76-89; D. Scott Hartwig, To Antietam Creek: The Maryland Campaign of 1862 (Baltimore: The Johns Hopkins University Press, 2012), 464-467; Brian Matthew Jordan, Unholy Sabbath: The Battle of South Mountain in History and Memory, September 14, 1862 (El Dorado Hills: Savas Beatie, 2012), 285.

starting point, with waysides describing the defensive line of the 15th North Carolina along the Arnoldstown Road, which intersects Gapland Road at the gap, and the two guns of the Troup Artillery—Sallie Craig and Jennie— deployed in the gap to stem the Yankee tide. Unleashing canister from the intersection at close range, the two Confederate pieces momentarily stunned the advancing Federals coming out of the woods. With scores of enemy rifles leveled at them, however, the Confederate cannoneers could not stay for long. In the withdrawal down the western side of the mountain, one of the guns became disabled and had to be left behind. Franklin's men held the gap by nightfall and continued into Pleasant Valley, but their efforts to get to Harpers Ferry would have to wait until the sun next rose. The next day a New Jersey soldier wrote that "I never was so near worn out as I was on the 14th when I was climing [sic] the side of the mountain and my face all black with powder." Hiking the loop trail at Crampton's Gap offers a hint of that experience.[197]

The loop trail at Crampton's Gap is located at the intersection of Gapland Road and Arnoldtown Road. N 39.405749, W 77.639576. The Appalachian Trail passes through Crampton's Gap at that location.

197 Hartwig, *To Antietam Creek*, 468-70.

Institute Interview: Sitting Down with Keith Snyder
by Laura Marfut

Antietam National Battlefield Park Ranger Keith Snyder considers his position as Chief of Resource Education and Visitor Services one of the best jobs in the world. He has made his mark on visitor experiences at four different parks since his career with the National Park Service began in 1985; perhaps none as profound as the ongoing redesign and renovation of Antietam National Battlefield's Visitor Center. In this interview, Keith shares the vision and concepts behind this project and other recent battlefield improvements, along with some special experiences at Antietam.

Keith is a graduate of Shepherd University and received his master's degree from the U. S. Army War College. For many years, his career with the National Park Service ran concurrently with a career in the United States Air Force and Air National Guard. He retired from the military as a colonel in 2016 after 40 years of service.

LM: There have been several major projects at Antietam recently. What has changed between old and new?

KS: A great deal of work has been done in the last couple years at the Burnside Bridge area. First was the restoration project of the bridge itself, then repairs and improvements to all the patios and sidewalks. A railing was added to make the walkway from the William McKinley monument much safer. Other projects include a rehabilitation of the Observation Tower. It was built in 1896 by the U.S. War Department and work was done to the stairs, railings, and stonework. A safety railing was added to the top level. Work continues at many of the historic farmsteads, and we are in the middle of a four-year project to improve our trail system. All this effort is part of implementing the park's vision that was established in our 2020 Strategic Plan: "Maintain Antietam National Battlefield as a sustainable historic landscape and tell stories in innovative ways that resonate with all people."

LM: The Visitor Center renovation is currently underway and

scheduled for completion in the fall of 2022. What will change?

KS: The Visitor Center project is monetarily the largest project in the history of the park with an expenditure of approximately $7 million. The key elements of this project are to make the building and the area around it more accessible and to modernize the facility. It was originally built in 1962 and over the years numerous problems have developed that we are addressing. For example, raw sewage from the failing septic system would back up into the lobby a couple times a year. Also, the roof leaked and the HVAC systems were inefficient. We are correcting all of those. The utilities will move to the basement and the staff will move to the main floor. The building is listed on the National Register of Historic Sites, so it is important to keep what are called the "character defining features" of the building, like the stonework, while modernizing it. Other key improvements include a new, full-size elevator to all three levels and solar panels on the roof.

LM: For visitors to Antietam, the transition to the temporary Visitor Center appeared relatively seamless. What challenges did you face?

KS: We are extremely pleased with our temporary building. The first challenge was getting it here from Georgia. It consists of seven trailers bolted together. Then we had to make sure the building was safe for staff and visitors before moving in. We moved in last July, the busiest month of the year. Luckily, we were able to re-use many of the interpretive panels from the historic visitor center. We added a few new panels and re-used our information desk. With COVID subsiding we were also able to open a theater room and re-use our audio-visual equipment to show our film in the temporary center. There are still some visitors who are confused about where to go, but we have improved that with signage and a new flag on the building.

LM: The new museum will feature exhibits centered around five themes, or "universal concepts." How were those concepts developed?

KS: One of the first things that we did in the planning process was to create a diverse and experienced Historians Advisory Team to help guide us. Our team included the current and the former Chief Historians of the National Park Service, senior Rangers, and educators from other Civil War parks. Leading academic historians experienced in Civil War and 19th Century history added to a park staff that had a combined experience of over 100 years working at Antietam. We locked ourselves in a room at the National Conversation Training Center in Shepherdstown, West Virginia, with our design team. We spent three days developing our themes, goals, and interpretive framework for the exhibits. One of our goals was to make our story relatable to all segments of society, which led to our use of what we call universal concepts to organize the space and guide the understanding of the battle and its legacy. The point of these concepts is that anyone can relate on some level to their meaning. The organizing concepts for the museum are conflict, terror, survival, freedom, and memory.

LM: What is the primary reason for updating the exhibits at this point in time?

KS: Some of our exhibit cases were fifty years old and it just made sense that, with the complete rehabilitation of the building, we should upgrade the exhibits at the same time. In addition, we wanted to improve our interpretation with the latest scholarship currently available. A great deal of new research has been completed recently about the Maryland Campaign and the causes and consequences of the Civil War.

LM: How will the new exhibits enhance the visitor experience at Antietam?

KS: Our approach is to use the entire Visitor Center experience to provide orientation and inspiration to then explore the battlefield and to act as a springboard to the resource. In other words, we want to prepare visitors with a better understanding of why two armies came to these fields to destroy each other, what happened when they arrived, and what the impact was on the soldiers and the community. Just as important for our story is the direct tie to the Emancipation Proclamation and how the park itself was created and preserved. The Visitor Center is the most appropriate space to introduce these ideas. Once out on the battlefield, we pivot to focus more on the specific people and events of the battle, on the actual locations where actions took place. Our goal is to be as site specific as possible on the resource that we preserve and protect.

LM: What is the meaning of the sculpture that will be featured in the new plaza leading up to the Visitor Center entrance?

KS: The sculpture that we have planned was a collaborative effort between the interpretive staff and our design team. It depicts an actual event that took place in the Cornfield. Sergeant William Paul of the 90th Pennsylvania Infantry and an unknown Confederate soldier fought hand to hand for control of the unit's National flag. Paul received the Medal of Honor for his actions.[198] We feel that this struggle for the colors

---

198 Paul's Medal of Honor citation is as follows: "The President of the United States of America, in the name of Congress, takes pleasure in presenting the Medal of

symbolizes the struggle for the nation. In addition, we have a quote etched into the sculpture, "Exposed to the fire of slavery and freedom." This was from a letter written by Private Julius F. Rabardy, Company K, 12th Massachusetts Infantry. Just yards away from William Paul's struggle, he was shot by Confederates and his own men. Our hope is that this piece of art will help establish in visitors' minds the meaning of the enormous struggle that took place here. Add to that our Civil War timeline which will be embedded into the sidewalk, and people should get some understanding of when and why this battle took place before they ever enter the building.

LM: Once the Visitor Center project is complete, what's next?

KS: The next major project for the Interpretive Division, which we have already started, is the creation of a new park film for our theater and a video wall production for the redesigned lobby of the Visitor Center. The park is extremely fortunate to be able to plan and execute the creation and installation of almost all aspects of a visitor's experience simultaneously. This is a rare opportunity, and it has created a synergy of research, design, and interpretation that we hope will increase everyone's personal and emotional connections to this special and unique place.

LM: What are the most important concepts you want visitors to take with them after a day at Antietam?

KS: First and foremost is to make sure people are welcomed and comfortable. It is also important to remember that most of our park visitors come here once in their lifetime and only have about two hours to spend, so it is important to be efficient with our interpretive efforts. Some folks just want to take a quick look, others like to read every word, so we must design for that, too. Our new exhibits are an example. We have the five large panels with our five universals or most important concepts. If someone just reads those in a few minutes, that will at least capture the essence of the battlefield. However, our exhibits also include quotes and key chronological and statistical information throughout, for those who want that kind of detail. For the first time, we are also creating ten different interactive exhibits to increase potential involvement and create different types of learning opportunities. With all that being said,

---

Honor to Private William H. Paul, United States Army, for extraordinary heroism on September 17, 1862, while serving with Company E, 90th Pennsylvania Infantry, in action at Antietam, Maryland. Under a most withering and concentrated fire, Private Paul voluntarily picked up the colors of his regiment, when the bearer and two of the color guards had been killed, and bore them aloft throughout the entire battle."

I would be happy if people walked away knowing that Antietam was the bloodiest one-day battle in American history; the Federal victory led directly to President Abraham Lincoln's issuance of the preliminary Emancipation Proclamation; and that this historic and commemorative landscape should be preserved forever.

LM: Have your dual careers with the National Park Service and Air Force Reserves complemented each other?

KS: I like to think so. Having a diversity of training, work and leadership experiences would seem to have provided me with different skills and perspectives that I might not have had otherwise. For me, communication and building relationships have been critical in both careers. I have also been extremely blessed to have worked at four National Parks while at the same time being assigned to numerous military positions, including spending a year at the U.S. Army War College in Carlisle, Pennsylvania. I have been fortunate to serve with, and for, some great leaders in both careers who have mentored me along the way. Not many people can say they have had the two best jobs in the world, both in service to the country. I strongly believe in the value of public service.

LM: What are some of the highlights of your tenure as Chief of Resource Education and Visitor Services at Antietam?

KS: When you have been here as long as I have, there are many special experiences and memories. It is hard to narrow them down to a few that I can share here. However, all of my greatest moments revolve around experiencing the battlefield and sharing our story with visitors. One of my best days was spending four hours with 17 four-star generals, including the Chairman of the Joint Chiefs of Staff, every Service Chief, and every Combatant Commander. One of my most rewarding and emotional days was a tour that I provided for the Make a Wish Foundation. I will never forget the young man and his family that I shared our story with. Each year, I love spending the morning with the Sharpsburg Elementary School fifth grade class who place over 5,000 flags in our National Cemetery for Memorial Day. Our Battle Anniversary sunrise program, the 150th Anniversary, touring the entire Kennedy family around the park with author Shelby Foote, being a pall bearer for the unknown New York Soldier, all are profound memories for me. But most importantly, the greatest highlights of my career are the exceptional people that I have an opportunity to work with. I never cease to be amazed at the dedication, pride, professionalism, and friendship demonstrated by the park staff that I am blessed to share this special place with.

Book Review

Welker, David A. *The Cornfield: Antietam's Bloody Turning Point.*
Philadelphia: Casemate Publishers, 2020. Hardcover, 26 maps, photos,
notes, bibliography, index. ISBN: 978-1-6120-0832-5. $34.95.

Review by James A. Rosebrock

There has been a need for an in-depth and objective battle narrative that
focuses on the Antietam Cornfield and incorporates the plans, execution,
and impact of the Cornfield fight on subsequent actions at the Battle of
Antietam. David Welker, at last, delivers that work. Mr. Welker is a
professional historian for the U.S. Government and the author of two
other highly regarded books: *Tempest at Ox Hill: The Battle of
Chantilly* and *A Keystone Rebel: The Diary of Joseph Garey.*

Mr. Welker begins with a thought-provoking analysis of Maj. Gen.
George B. McClellan's approach to planning the Battle of Antietam.
There is much for the reader to think about here. Welker offers that in
McClellan's thought process, reason, not emotion or intuition, should
guide decision-making. He refutes popular assertions that McClellan was
not a risk-taker and in fact demonstrates that McClellan believed that

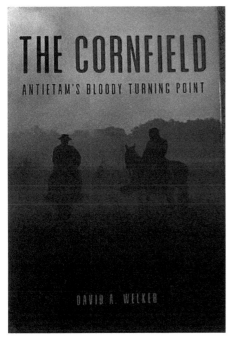

great things entail great risks. An
example is the Peninsula Campaign
where McClellan put his army on
ships and undertook a risky
flanking maneuver against
uncertain landing conditions and
unknown enemy positions.
McClellan mitigates and manages
great risks by deliberate, thorough
planning. In the dynamic and
changing situation of the tactical
battlefield, however, Welker
submits that McClellan's style of
command amounted to little more
than managing the battle and
reacting to events, not taking the
initiative and steering events in a
path necessary to reach victory.

This may be a more controversial stance, but Mr. Welker's position is worth reading and considering.

Chapter Two is an excellent telling of the road to Antietam and the maneuvers of both armies to Sharpsburg during the first two weeks of September 1862. The tight, crisp description of the opposing army's moves and countermoves in 15 pages is highly valuable and a clear summary of the leadup to America's bloodiest day. The author believes that General Lee misjudged the Federal response to his entering Maryland. Like many students of the battle, he characterizes the discovery of Special Orders No. 191 as an "intelligence windfall." Other recent scholarship by historians like Steven Stotelmyer rebut this position and offers that the measures that McClellan took on September 14 were the result of orders and plans directed the day before and that at the most, the lost orders merely verified McClellan's perception of Lee's plans. The author's well written account of the lead up to the battle is excellent.

The author refutes assertions by some historians that McClellan "telegraphed" his move in crossing the Upper Bridge under the noses of observing Confederate cavalry on the afternoon of September 16. He asserts that McClellan *wanted* Lee to know about the move, compelling the Confederate command to move troops from other parts of the line. Hooker's objective was not to defeat the entire Confederate army but to occupy the Dunker Church plateau. With another attack by Maj. Gen. Ambrose Burnside's Ninth Corps on the southern flank, the author maintains General McClellan's main attack was to be against Lee's center. Here Welker describes the main attack to be by Federal troops of the Fifth and Sixth corps. In fact, the original plan called for the Second and Fifth corps to make the attack, with the Sixth corps acting as a reserve when it arrived from Rohrersville.

Mr. Welker introduces a fascinating concept of intermediate goals. For Hooker to reach his primary goal of the Dunker Church, he had to capture the two intermediate goals of the Cornfield and the East Woods which were a salient pushed forward by "Stonewall" Jackson. The author contributes a new concept to battlefield scholarship here which will be the subject of much conversation by students of the Maryland Campaign who seek out this book.

The heart of this book is the detailed battlefield narrative of the action in the Cornfield. Welker unpacks the fighting in the Cornfield in a very impactful and effective way. He paints a clear visual image of the Cornfield area as a tactical box surrounded by woodlots to the north, west, and east. This characterization is another new idea that students of the Maryland Campaign will certainly further discuss and analyze. What I found to be particularly valuable throughout the book is Welker's constant insertion of date and time stamps that allow the reader to know where and when he is at all times in the action.

Welker examines the actions in minute detail from the preliminary movements during the night before the main action through all of the back-and-forth punches and counterpunches of the rival armies. We accompany the combatants and through their compelling and powerful first-hand accounts, observe leadership, bravery and cowardice, and experience the terrible sights, sounds, smells, pain, and visceral terror of the bloody Cornfield.

There is often a tendency for writers who cover the entire battle, to move past the Cornfield after Hood's attack. Welker however avoids this and rightly spends the necessary time and detail discussing the arrival of Brig. Gen. Joseph Mansfield's Twelfth Corps and credits (rightly) the role of Brig. Gen. Alpheus Williams in turning the tide of the Cornfield fight. We see the arrival and repulse of Maj. Gen. John Sedgwick's division, Greene's advance to the Dunker Church, and finally, the expedition by Maj. Gen. J.E.B. Stuart at the end of the day to turn the Federal right flank.

The book is deeply researched and uses 75 manuscript and unpublished works as well as over 200 published sources.

A few spelling errors ("Calvalry" in the list of maps) and dates (1962 instead of 1862) are very minor distractions. On the artillery side, however, the author describes the Federal guns of position as "dozens of batteries lining the eastern bank of the Antietam [that] had opened without any apparent reason other than to join the growing bombardment." In fact, a count of the batteries on Ezra Carman's maps shows the number of batteries to range around ten. On page 24, where he describes the Federal wing structure, he places Burnside on the left and Franklin on the right when it was the other way around.

The Cornfield: Antietam's Bloody Turning Point is a satisfying read that tells the story of the climactic fight for the Cornfield clearly and compellingly. It should be on the bookshelf of every student of the Maryland Campaign.

Contributor Biographies

Richard P. D'Ambrisi has been an American Civil War civilian living historian and museum docent since 1986. He has developed mid-19th century characterizations for an apothecary, phrenologist, railroad worker and baseball player that have been presented at Civil War reenactments, vintage baseball tournaments, museums, and historic sites. He is a Certified Interpretive Guide with the National Association for Interpretation.

Kevin R. Pawlak is the editor of *The Antietam Journal*. He serves as an Antietam Battlefield Guide and is the author of five books, including *To Hazard All: A Guide to the Maryland Campaign, 1862*.

Russell Rich is an Antietam Battlefield Guide. He graduated from the University of Virginia with a Bachelor of Arts degree in History.

Joseph Stahl retired from the Institute for Defense Analyses. He is active in the Civil War community and has authored more than two dozen articles. Most recently, he authored *Faces of Union Soldiers at South Mountain & Harpers Ferry*.

J.O. Smith has a master's degree in history from the University of Georgia and undergraduate and law degrees from Duke University. He is an attorney and lives with his family near Annapolis, Maryland. He has been a Certified Antietam Battlefield Guide since 2018.

Laura Marfut is a retired U.S. Army colonel with master's degrees in International Relations and Education, and a Master of Strategic Studies degree from the U.S. Army War College. She has been a Certified Antietam Battlefield Guide since 2019.

James A. Rosebrock is a retired Army officer and Department of Justice employee. Jim has two Civil War-related blogs and is currently completing *Artillery of Antietam*, due for release in 2022.

Antietam Institute Membership Honor Roll

Corporate Members

Special thanks to all our Corporate Members!
Your support provides essential funding to help us sustain and grow educational programs and publications that are the foundation of the Institute.

Antietam Mercantile Company
138 W. Main Street
Sharpsburg, MD 21782
facebook.com/AntietamMercantile
240-310-4011

Bonnie's at The Red Byrd
19409 Shepherdstown Pike
Keedysville, MD 21756
facebook.com/Bonniesattheredbyrd
301-432-5822

The Inn at Antietam
220 East Main Street
Sharpsburg, MD 21782
innatantietam.com
301-432-6601

Jacob Rohrbach Inn
138 W. Main Street
Sharpsburg, MD 21782
jacob-rohrbach-inn.com
301-432-5079

Antietam Creek Vineyards
4835 Branch Ave,
Sharpsburg, MD 21782
antietamcreekvineyards.com
240-490-2851

Honor Guard Members
(Life-time members)

Mac Bryan
Matthew Borders
Lucas Cade
Mike Crume
Rogers M. Fred, III
Bradley M. Gottfried
Robert Gottschalk
Bruce Gourley
Michael Kirschner
William Lowe
Laura Marfut
Mike McCartney
Colleen McMillan
Tom McMillan
Sharon Murray
Keith O'Neil
Kevin Pawlak
Scottie Riffle
Gary Rohrer
Jim Rosebrock
Austin Slater
Scott & Kate Shaffer
Clayton Tucker
Doug Valentine
Chris & Amy Vincent
Darin & Jan Wipperman
Charles Young

Honorary Colonel Members
Randy Short

Honorary Captain Members
Gordon Dammann
Judi McHugh
Sid White

As of July 1, 2022

☐ **New Member**   ☐ **Renewal**

NAME: _____   HOME PHONE: (___) _____

EMAIL ADDRESS: _____   CELL PHONE: (___) _____

MAILING ADDRESS: _____

CITY: _____   STATE: _____   ZIP CODE: _____

Preferred method of communication: ☐ email   ☐ phone   ☐ post

Please select your Membership Level (benefits are listed on reserves side form):

☐ Cadet - $10 (Student)   ☐ *Lieutenant - $250
☐ Private - $25   ☐ *Captain - $350
☐ Corporal - $50   ☐ *Colonel - $500
☐ Sergeant - $75   ☐ *Honor Guard (Life Member) - $1000
☐ *Sergeant Major - $150   ☐ Sutler – Business Sponsor- $500

*Please select shirt size: SM ☐   MD ☐   LG ☐   XL ☐   2XL ☐   3XL ☐

Please select Style: Men's ☐   Women's ☐

PLEASE MAKE CHECK PAYABLE TO: Antietam Institute
P.O. Box 33
Sharpsburg, MD 21782

How did you hear about the Antietam Institute?

_____

Through your membership the Antietam Institute will be able to support the Antietam National Battlefield and other local preservation and historical organizations. Your membership will also entitle you to attend Institute events as well as discounted publications and merchandise. The Institute is a tax-exempt, public benefit, non-profit corporation and qualifies under Section 501(c)(3) of the IRS code. Your membership and donations are tax-deductible as allowed by law.

If you have any questions or need additional information, contact our Membership at:
antietaminstitutemembership@gmail.com

Cadet - $10 (Student, under 21 in school)
- 10% discount on all Antietam Institute merchandise and events.

Private - $25
- 10% discount on all Antietam Institute merchandise

Corporal - $50
- Same benefits as Private Level
- Subscription to our bi-annual "Antietam Journal"

Sergeant - $75
- Same benefits as Corporal Level
- Antietam Institute logo hat

Sergeant Major - $150
- Same benefits as Sergeant Level
- Antietam Institute logo polo shirt
- *Exclusive offer - copy of the *Artillery Units of Antietam* (available for a limited time only)

Lieutenant - $250
- Same benefits as Sergeant Major Level
- 25% discount to the annual Symposium or Conference
- *Exclusive offer - copy of the Artillery Units of Antietam (available for a limited time only)

Captain - $350
- Same benefits as Lieutenant Level
- 25% discount to the annual Spring Symposium
- 25% discount to the annual Fall Conference
- Recognition as an "Honorary Captain" member in the *"Antietam Journal"*
- *Exclusive offer - copy of the *Artillery Units of Antietam* (available for a limited time only)

Colonel - $500
- Same benefits as Captain Level
- Invitations to exclusive programs (Annual Honor Guard Gathering)
- Recognition as an "Honorary Colonel" member in the *"Antietam Journal"*
- *Exclusive offer - copy of the *Artillery Units of Antietam* (available for a limited time only)

Honor Guard-$1000 (Lifetime Member)
- 10% discount on all Antietam Institute merchandise
- Subscription to our bi-annual "Antietam Journal"
- Antietam Institute logo hat
- Antietam Institute logo polo shirt
- Invitations to exclusive programs (Annual Honor Guard Gathering)
- Recognition as an "Honor Guard" member in the *"Antietam Journal"*
- *Exclusive offer - copy of the BArtillery Units of Antietam (available for a limited time only)

Institute Sutler - Business Sponsor - $500
- Corporal level membership for Business owner, including complimentary pass to the Spring Symposium
- ¼ page advertisement in the "Antietam Journal" and in Institute event programs
- Recognition and company logo on the Antietam Institute website.
- Recognition as an "Honorary Sutler" in the "Antietam Journal"

Printed in the USA
CPSIA information can be obtained
at www.ICGtesting.com
LVHW060547031223
765362LV00028B/1834